TOP 10
CANCÚN AND THE YUCATÁN

CONTENTS

4

Introducing Cancún and the Yucatán

18

Top 10 Highlights

48

Top 10 of Everything

82

Area by Area

122

Streetsmart

CANCÚN AND THE YUCATÁN

INTRODUCING

A stretch of palm-fringed beach, Akumal

WELCOME TO CANCÚN AND THE YUCATÁN

Whether you want to enjoy sun, sea, and beach-club vibes, or immerse yourself in the Maya world, Cancún and the wider Yucatán have something special in store. Don't want to miss a thing? With Top 10 Cancún and the Yucatán you'll enjoy the very best the region has to offer.

The lush coastlines, ancient Maya sites, natural wonders, and lively party scene have combined to make the Yucatán a holiday haven. Its Riviera Maya, on the east coast, is dotted with towns like Cancún and Playa del Carmen, which, along with the islands of Cozumel and Isla Mujeres, draw all types of travelers to their idyllic stretches of sand and sea, luxurious

El Castillo Maya site, Tulum

resorts, and hedonistic nightlife. From here, you can easily explore the abundant natural beauty along the coast: dive amid the Mesoamerican Reef, the second-longest barrier reef in the world; take boat trips to peaceful coves and beaches; or spot wildlife at the Sian Ka'an Biosphere Reserve.

It's not all about the coast, though. Journey inland to uncover the other side of the region, filled with picture-postcard towns, dramatic cenotes, and world-famous Maya sites such as Chichén Itzá and Uxmal. You'll also find the colonial cities of Valladolid, Izamal, and Campeche, where the alluring architecture hints at the Yucatán's complex history, and Mérida, a melting pot of art, traditions, and fabulous food. It's in these areas that you'll see the unique Yucatecan identity – in dishes such as *cochinita pibil* (marinated pork), in the speech of the Maya and other Indigenous communities, and in local festivals. With so much to do, it's little wonder that writers have often described the Yucatán as a country within a country.

So, where to start? With Top 10 Cancún and the Yucatán, of course. This pocket-sized guide gets to the heart of the region with simple lists of 10, expert local knowledge, and comprehensive maps, helping you turn an ordinary trip into an extraordinary one.

THE STORY OF CANCÚN AND THE YUCATÁN

From the center of Maya civilization to a modern-day magnet for travelers from around the globe, the Yucatán tells a stirring story. Today, visible vestiges of the past now sit alongside the ever-growing shoots of modernity. Here's the story of how it came to be.

First Settlers

Habitation in the Yucatán Peninsula, which comprises parts of Mexico, Belize, and Guatemala, dates back to before 10,000 BCE. Little is known until 2000 BCE when the Maya people, who would dominate for thousands of years, settled here. The early millennia, known as the Preclassic Period (2000 BCE–250 CE), saw an evolution from simple settlements to complex cities, centered in the south of the peninsula. Alongside this, there were remarkable scientific and cultural advances, which included books made from fig trees, a hieroglyphic writing system, and a 365-day calendar.

The Maya Civilization

In the first centuries CE, the Maya civilization collapsed in the south and power moved north, to the modern-day Yucatán and Quintana Roo regions. This coincided with the start of a centuries-long boom, known as the Classic Period (250–900 CE). This era was defined by a cultural flowering in cosmology, mathematics, and calendrics, as well as the construction of magnificent cities and temples, such as Tikal and Palenque.

Yet, around 900 CE, the Maya experienced a sudden collapse. Archaeologists are still puzzled as to why this happened, with theories ranging from political infighting to climate change. In the era that followed, known as the Postclassic Period (900–1500 CE), the region was beset by war and many cities were abandoned in favor of more defendable settlements. The center of power moved further north, and for a time,

A fresco from the Temple of the Warriors at Chichén Itzá

An artistic depiction of the Maya city of Uxmal

local sites in this area, such as Chichén Itzá, Uxmal, and Mayapán, continued to flourish. Eventually, though, these also collapsed, and by the 16th century the Maya were reduced to isolated settlements without a central authority.

Spanish Colonization

The traditional Maya way of life was upended by the arrival of Spanish explorers in 1517. The first expeditions under Francisco Hernández de Córdoba (1517), Juan de Grijalva (1518), and Hernán Cortés (1519) made small incursions and little headway, but in 1527, the Spanish launched a full conquest under conquistador Francisco de Montejo. His first two invasions (the second in 1531) resulted in little success due to strong Maya resistance, with heavy losses for both sides. But the Maya were also decimated by European diseases and de Montejo capitalized on this during his third invasion, in 1540. By 1546, many Maya chiefs had been defeated or peacefully submitted, and the Spanish-governed cities of Mérida and Valladolid had been established. Total victory remained elusive, however: no Maya authority meant no official surrender. In late 1546, several communities rose up during the Great Maya Revolt, attacking Valladolid in a period of tumult that took months to subdue.

Moments in History

2000 BCE
The Yucatán's first Maya inhabitants establish early settlements and begin to cultivate crops, including the "three sisters": maize, beans, and squash.

2000 BCE–250 CE
Maya culture establishes itself in earnest during the Preclassic Period, with the rise of the first cities.

250–900
The Classic Period of Maya civilization, which sees the founding of magnificent cities and scientific developments.

900
The start of the Postclassic Period, which lasts until 1500, marks the sudden decline of Maya power in the south.

1517
Francisco Hernández de Córdoba's expedition reaches the Yucatán, marking the first contact between the Maya and Spanish conquistadors.

1821
Mexico declares its independence from Spain. The Yucatán Peninsula is initially divided about whether it will join the new republic, but eventually does so.

1847–1901
The Caste War, a series of Maya uprisings against exploitation of ruling elites, causes widespread unrest and kills many hundreds of thousands.

1971
The government invests heavily in tourism, and the first hotel opens in Cancún, marking the start of the international tourist boom.

2012
The "end of the world," when the long cycle of the Maya calendar draws to a close, brining thousands of visitors to the region.

2024
The ambitious but controversial *Tren Maya* opens, promising a boost to tourism but raising questions about environmental impact.

Colonial Rule

After quelling the revolt, colonial rule was established and the Spanish set about exploiting the locals, instituting slave-like conditions for workers and sending Catholic missionaries to convert the locals and end Indigenous practices. Such oppressive policies increased trade and commerce but also led to several uprisings during the 17th and 18th centuries, most notably the Canek Rebellion of 1761, which resulted in the execution of insurgents and the burning of the town of Cisteil.

Revolution and Independence

Despite the reaction to the Canek Rebellion, resentment continued to fester across Mexico and eventually led to the end of Spanish rule, through the Mexican War of Independence (1810–1821). There was broad support for this movement across the Yucatán and key battles were fought here. After independence was achieved in 1821, the regional administration grudgingly joined the newly formed Mexico. The Yucatán elites had designs on forming an independent nation, and these early decades were marked by multiple attempts to break away from the nascent government in Mexico City. Such efforts were halted in 1847, when a Maya uprising against the Yucateos (the European-descended elite) started what became known as the Caste War (1847–1901). The Maya established a

A painted depiction of a battle during the Caste War

Visitors exploring the towering ruins of El Castillo, Tulum

near-independent state in the southeast of the region and fought bloody battles against the Mexican forces, during which hundreds of thousands were killed. Though the main battles occurred in the first years of the conflict, the war dragged on until 1901 and was only ended by the occupation of the rebel capital Chan Santa Cruz.

From Henequen to Tourism

In spite of the conflict, the Yucatán had become Mexico's wealthiest state in the late 19th century thanks to a boom in the henequen industry, used primarily for sisal rope. The economic growth brought new wealth, reflected in the extravagant mansions in Mérida, and the Mexican government took steps to modernize and develop the region. This boom proved short-lived, and by 1910, the industry had collapsed and the area receded into an isolated backwater.

The Yucatán was only awoken from its slumber in the 1950s, when the region was finally connected to the rest of Mexico by rail, and subsequently road. Quickly, the area's potential for tourism was realized and in the decades that followed, the government pumped massive amounts of money into the area's infrastructure. Splashy marketing campaigns focused on its beautiful beaches and plethora of Maya sites, and the first hotel in Cancún opened in 1971. By the 1980s, the Yucatán had become an international travel hot spot and tourism was now a major source of employment for many locals.

Cancún and the Yucatán Today

Tourism in the Yucatán has gone from strength to strength, and with places like Cancún, Playa del Carmen, and Cozumel among the most popular destinations in Mexico, it is now arguably the most important part of the local economy. This tourism boom has in turn spurred new, evermore ambitious projects to increase both revenue and visitors to the state. The most notable (and controversial) of these is the *Tren Maya*, a passenger train inaugurated in late 2024. Its negative impact on the environment and traditional culture has fueled debate on the region's future and the importance of tourism to the Yucatan's economic fortunes.

TOP 10 EXPERIENCES

Planning the perfect trip to Cancún and the Yucatán? Whether you're visiting for the first time or making a return trip, there are some things you simply shouldn't miss out on. To make the most of your time – and to enjoy the very best this region has to offer – be sure to add these experiences to your list.

1 Dance the night away

This is Mexico's party capital, where revelers from across the world go to blow off steam. The party town of Playa del Carmen has all-night events at the likes of Mandala *(p91)* while Cancún is packed with numerous mega-clubs, including the cavernous Coco Bongo and the ice-filled Amma Club *(p91)*.

2 Experience Cancún and the Yucatán's beaches

You can't come to the Yucatán without visiting the beach. The sun-drenched coast has some of Mexico's best sandy beaches *(p56)*, many with crystalline waters to swim in. It doesn't get any better than soaking in the sun while sipping a refreshing cocktail.

3 Go island-hopping

While there's plenty to keep you busy on the mainland, the Yucatán's eye-catching islands are certainly worth a side trip. Cozumel *(p24)* may be the most popular, but Isla Holbox *(p85)* and Isla Mujeres *(p30)* are also excellent. All are quieter than Cancún and have miles of golden beaches to explore.

4 Visit Maya sites

The Yucatán is home to some of the world's finest archaeological sites, all preserved since the ancient Maya civilization ruled the region. Take in the elegant city of Uxmal *(p42)*, the seaside majesty of Tulum *(p32)*, or the pyramids at Chichén Itzá *(p36)*, the most famous Maya site in Mexico.

5 Go bird-watching

Whether you're a serious twitcher or a casual bird-watcher, the Yucatán's 550 avian species make it an ideal place to spot birds. Tour the many eco-parks *(p60)* and wildlife reserves *(p62)*, or jump in a tour boat to reach the American flamingos' habitat in Celestún *(p63)*.

6 Take a dip in a cenote

The Yucatán's thousands of natural sinkholes are among the world's great marvels. These cenotes *(p64)* were sacred to the Maya, but today the still waters are perfect for swimming. A good first-timer's choice is practically under Restaurante Zací *(p113)*, in Valladolid.

7 Sleep in a historic hacienda

The Yucatán was once filled with fabulous hacienda estates producing henequen. Many still have their original features and have been reborn as opulent hotels, with Hacienda San José Cholul *(p132)* and Hacienda Temozón Sur *(p133)* among the best.

8 Go wild at Sian Ka'an Biosphere Reserve

The Sian Ka'an Biosphere Reserve *(p34)* is one of the Yucatán's true treasures, a seriously huge refuge for hundreds of animal species and over 1,000 species of plants. Tours by land or water offer incredible experiences.

9 Enjoy Mérida's festivities

The capital of the Yucatán is always charming, but time your visit with a festival *(p80)* to make it truly memorable. Whether it's January's Mérida Fest, the biggest regional carnival; Day of the Dead; or the weekly Mérida en Domingo *(p81)*, you're guaranteed a good time.

10 Savor signature dishes

Every region of Mexico has distinct flavors and the Yucatán is no exception, with its hearty meat dishes, smoky and spicy flavors, and Maya influences. Take your pick from simple soups, fantastic street food, fried fish along the coast, and Maya staples *(p74)*.

ITINERARIES

Visiting majestic Maya sites, relaxing on white sandy beaches, partying all night long: there's a lot to see and do in Cancún and the Yucatán. With places to eat and drink, these itineraries offer ways to spend 4 days and 7 days in the region.

4 DAYS

Day 1

Where better to start your adventure than in Cancún itself. Spend a couple of hours at the excellent Museo Maya de Cancún *(p23)*, learning about the Maya heritage of the area. Make sure to visit the San Miguelito Maya complex, located here, which has fascinating structures, including the five-story Chaak Palace, at its center. Hop over to the cozy El Pabilo *(p92)* for an early lunch, which will give you time for an afternoon trip to one of the area's more unique sites, the Museo Subacuático de Arte *(p22)*. Choose from a glass-bottom boat, snorkeling, or diving tour of this unique underwater sculpture museum (afternoon tours depart at 1pm or 2pm and last at least a couple of hours). As evening arrives, enjoy the sunset on Playa Delfines *(p89)* and a dinner of classic Maya dishes at La Parrilla *(p93)*, before partying at Coco Bongo *(p91)*.

Relaxing in a beachfront pool at Parque Garrafón

EAT

Looking for the best seafood in Cancún? Book a table at Fred's *(fredshouserestaurant.com)* and opt for the adobo chili lobster tail or the more expensive lobster thermidor, served in a wooden treasure chest.

Day 2

Rise early and board the ferry from near Playa Tortugas to the paradisical Isla Mujeres *(p30)*. The ferry port is in the north of the island, so begin with a few hours in Isla Town *(p30)*, famous for its old-school feel and colorful buildings. Pop into Lola Valentina *(p92)* for a fresh cocktail and then hail a taxi to take you to Parque Garrafón *(p60)*. Lunch at the Joint Reggae Bar 'n Grill *(thejoint isla.com)* before an afternoon of fun activities – snorkeling, paddleboarding, kayaking, or ziplining – or relaxation with a *temazcal* treatment *(p60)*. Take a taxi and then a ferry back to Cancún for dinner at Kiosco Verde *(Av López Portillo SM. 84, Lotte 14)*. The octopus or stuffed lobster are recommended.

Day 3

Today is about arguably Mexico's most famous sites, Chichén Itzá *(p36)*, one of the "Seven New Wonders of the World." Chichén is two hours from Cancún by car, so it's best to either book an early private transfer or rent a car so that you can beat the tour groups that arrive by late morning. Visit the famous Castillo de Kukulcán pyramid early to enjoy the area in relative peace, before exploring the other pyramids, temples, and ball courts of this complex. Stop for a picnic lunch in the shadow of a monument. You can spend an entire day here, but Ik Kil Cenote *(p110)* is just two miles (3 km) away and the 155-ft- (48-m-) deep hole makes for a great afternoon swimming detour. Return to Cancún for a dinner of classic regional fare at Le Chique *(p93)*.

Performers soaring above crowds at Xcaret Eco-Park

Day 4

For your final day, hop in your rental or on the bus (ADO Bus Station) and head to Xcaret *(p28)*, a massive eco-park with a beautiful jungle setting. There's an incredible array of activities to do here, so spend your morning spotting rare wildlife, exploring coves and lagoons, or even walking along the bed of the Caribbean Sea. Once you've had your fill, head 4 miles (6 km) north, to Playa del Carmen, for a seafood meal at Las Brisas *(p93)*. Then it's time to take it easy with some retail therapy on the town's main avenue, Quinta Avenida *(p26)*, before catching some final rays on Town Beach *(p26)*. After the sun sets, head north to the Vidanta Mayan Palace *(p130)*, to enjoy dinner while watching the spectacular Cirque du Soleil JOYÀ show. A perfect way to end your trip.

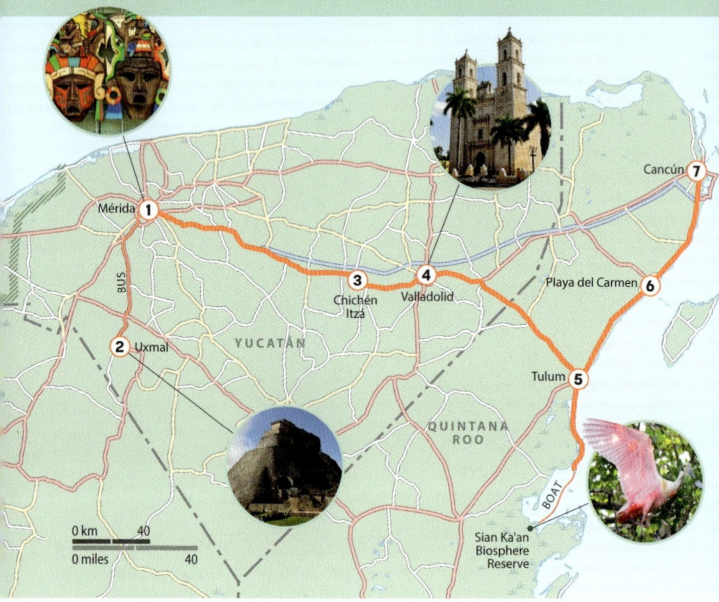

7 DAYS

Day 1

Kickstart your sojourn in the Yucatán's capital, Mérida *(p40)*. Get to know the city on a stroll around the historic *centro* district, visiting the colonial Palacio del Gobernador *(p40)* and the Catedral de San Ildefonso *(p40)*. Enjoy lunch at a spot on Paseo de Montejo *(p41)* before spending an afternoon learning about the Maya at the Museo de Antropología *(p41)*. As evening comes, sample traditional Yucatecan dishes at Ku'uk *(p120)* and then visit Plaza Mayor *(p40)*, where you might be serenaded by *tríos*.

Day 2

Hop on an early bus from the ADO Bus Station to visit one of the Yucatán's iconic Maya sites, the city of Uxmal *(p42)*. Allow at least the morning to wander around this incredible complex, which hints at what the Maya civilization once looked like. Return to Mérida for some shopping in Mérida Market *(p118)*, the perfect place to pick up a souvenir. Eat dinner, then stroll to El Cardenal Cantina *(p72)*, the oldest such bar in Mérida, to enjoy live music and some samba.

> **TRANSPORTATION**
> Mérida airport serves destinations within North America, but it may be easier, and cheaper, to fly to Cancún. If you do fly to Cancún, either reverse the route or add a day to the start of the trip and use the *Tren Maya (p124)* to reach Mérida.

Day 3

The Maya theme continues today, with a visit to Chichén Itzá *(p36)*. Pick up your rental car bright and early and make the 90-minute drive. A first visit is best enjoyed by hiring a knowledgeable local guide, who will help you understand the spiritual, political, and commercial significance of the place. When you've had your fill of Chichén, drive on to

Valladolid *(p108)*. Wander over to the city's main square, Parque Francisco Canton, where you may catch a troupe performing a traditional *jarana* dance.

Day 4

Grab breakfast and then set off on a walk or cycle around the city center. Take time to admire the colorful colonial architecture (particularly along Calzada de los Frailes) and visit the historic Convento San Bernardino de Siena *(p52)*. Afterward, go for a swim in the city's sinkhole, Cenote Zací, with lunch at the adjoining Restaurante Zací *(p113)*. Don't have dessert yet. Instead, visit the Choco Story museum *((999) 289 9914)* to learn about the importance of cacao in Maya culture – and, of course, enjoy a tasting. In the evening, drive on to Tulum *(p32)*.

Day 5

Today, it's all about nature at the vast Sian Ka'an Biosphere Reserve *(p34)*, the region's largest protected area, home to abundant wildlife and natural wonders. It's possible to drive there, but the roads are very poor, so a trip from Tulum with Sian Ka'an Tours *(siankaantours.org)* is the best option. All of their tours last several hours, but should still give you enough time to kick back on Playa Paraíso *(p32)*, after returning to Tulum.

Day 6

Give yourself a relaxed couple of hours at the Tulum Maya archaeological site *(p32)* this morning, working your way toward the imposing El Castillo *(p33)*, set upon a bluff. Leave Tulum behind and drive an hour north to the scenic Playa del Carmen *(p26)*. Here, you can shop along the town's Quinta Avenida *(p26)* and bask under the sun on INTI beach *(p26)*, with its beach club. After sunning yourself, drive an hour farther to reach your final stop, Cancún *(p22)*.

Day 7

Start your final day in Ciudad Cancún. Pick up some final souvenirs in the shops along Avenida Tulum *(p22)*, before mingling with locals in Mercardo 28 *(p90)*, a great place for lunch. Then it's back to the hotel zone for swimming and sunbathing on the beach off Boulevard Kukulcán *(p22)*. Scuba enthusiasts can book a trip to the offshore reefs with a local company. Complete your week with a Michelin-starred dinner at La Casa de los Mayoras *(p93)*, and a big night out in the clubs around the Corazón *(p23)*.

Leaning palm trees on Playa Paraíso, Tulum

TOP 10 HIGHLIGHTS

A painted stone panel at Chichén Itzá

EXPLORE THE **HIGHLIGHTS**

There are some sights in Cancún and the Yucatán you simply shouldn't miss, and it's these attractions that make the Top 10. Discover what makes each one a must-see on the following pages.

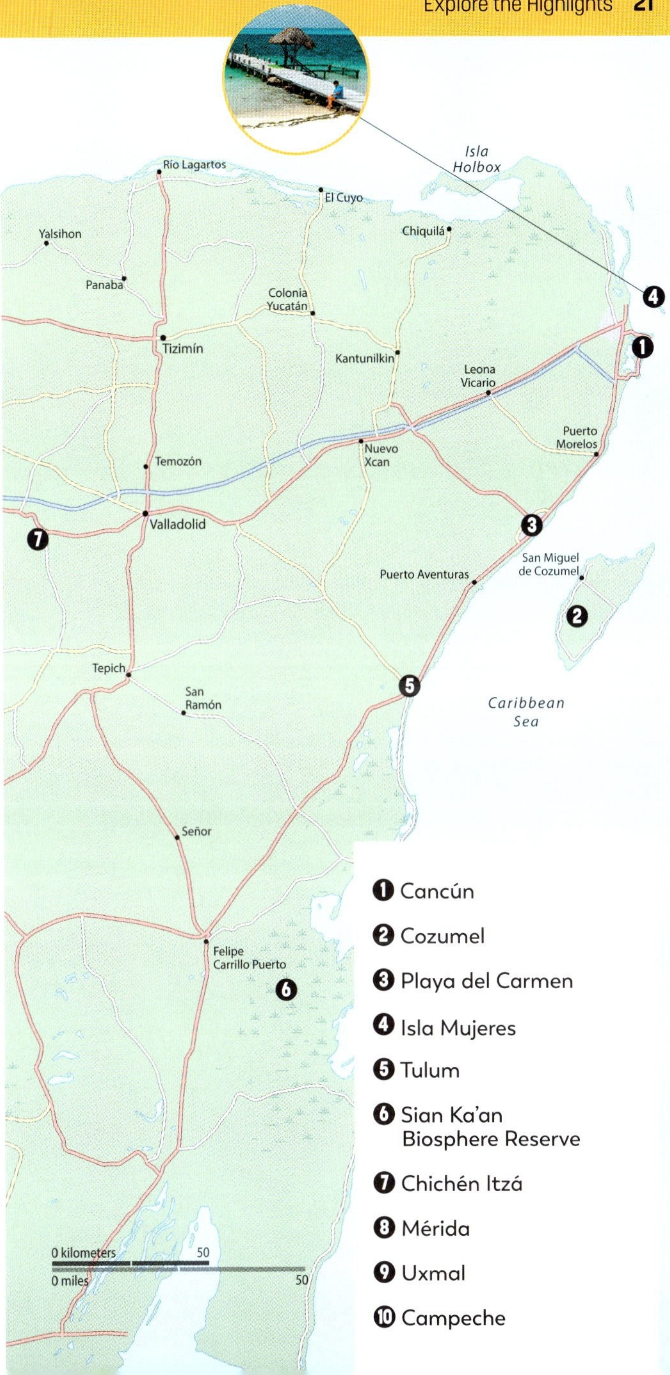

Isla Holbox
Río Lagartos
El Cuyo
Yalsihon
Chiquilá
Panaba
Colonia Yucatán
Tizimín
Kantunilkin
Leona Vicario
Puerto Morelos
Nuevo Xcan
Temozón
Valladolid
San Miguel de Cozumel
Puerto Aventuras
Tepich
San Ramón
Caribbean Sea
Señor
Felipe Carrillo Puerto
0 kilometers 50
0 miles 50

1. Cancún
2. Cozumel
3. Playa del Carmen
4. Isla Mujeres
5. Tulum
6. Sian Ka'an Biosphere Reserve
7. Chichén Itzá
8. Mérida
9. Uxmal
10. Campeche

1

CANCÚN

R2 Kiosks inside Town Hall; mexicancaribbean.travel

Just a dot on the map before 1970, Cancún is today the biggest resort in the Caribbean. Its Hotel Zone, centered on Boulevard Kukulcán, spans a long, narrow sand spit shaped like a giant "7," packed with hotels, shopping malls, restaurants, museums, and ancient Maya sites. On the mainland is the town of Ciudad Cancún, better known as Downtown.

1 The Beach

K4–K5

Cancún's main highlight is its beach, which is made up of fine white silicate sand that remains cool despite the warmth of the sun. It can be reached via several public access points from Boulevard Kukulcán.

2 Shopping Areas

A shopaholic's dream, Cancún offers everything from Mexican souvenirs in the markets of Downtown to international fashion in the Hotel Zone's vast, gleaming malls, including the exclusive waterside shopping center, La Isla *(p90)*.

3 Avenida Tulum and Downtown

The hub of the more Mexican part of Ciudad Cancún is tree-lined Avenida Tulum. It's a good spot for a stroll, and its cafés and restaurants are far quieter than those by the beach.

4 Laguna Nichupté

K4

This placid lagoon, enclosed by Cancún Island, offers more tranquility than the ocean, and is a favorite place for watersports. To the west are mangroves and jungle.

Cancún's palm-fringed beach

A GROWING RESORT

In the late 1960s, the Mexican government decided to transform this area into the country's first resort. Until then, the island was uninhabited. The first hotel, now the Dreams Hotel, opened at Punta Cancún in 1971. Since then, Cancún has acquired over 35,000 hotel rooms, attracting over 12 million visitors every year.

EAT

Sample the best local street food at the lively stalls and restaurants around the famous Mercado 28 *(p90)* in Downtown.

5 MUSA (Museo Subacuático de Arte)

Over 500 statues, created by British sculptor Jason deCaires Taylor, can be viewed via scuba-diving, snorkeling, or on a glass-bottomed boat at this incredible underwater sculpture park.

6 Museo Maya de Cancún

K5 Blvd Kukulcán, km 16.5 9am–5pm Wed–Mon granmuseodelmundomaya.com.mx

This beautiful museum is dedicated to the learning about the ancient Maya civilization. Right next to the striking modern building that houses it is an archaeological site called San Miguelito with plenty to explore.

7 Ventura Park

J6 Blvd Kukulcán, km 25 10am–5pm daily venturapark.com

This water park has slides and rides of all sizes for all ages, a snorkeling pool with stingrays and (harmless) sharks, and even bungee-jumping.

8 El Meco Site

Near the Isla Mujeres ferry ports, the city of El Meco *(p88)* dates back to 300 CE. It has a majestic pyramid and the remains of a Maya palace.

9 El Rey Site

These structures *(p88)* were part of a city that was prominent in the last centuries of Maya civilization, just before the Spanish invasion. Close to the site is a re-creation of a Maya village, where visitors can get an insight into the Maya way of life, including traditional cooking styles.

10 Nighttime Cancún

Cancún's nightlife is most concentrated in the "Corazón" but it extends all the way to Ciudad Cancún. A nonstop party atmosphere is maintained in clubs varying from Mexican traditional to modern cool.

Artifacts in the Museo Maya de Cancún

COZUMEL

R5 Av 5a sur 51

The island of Cozumel was the first part of the Yucatán to become internationally popular after the famous oceanographer Jacques Cousteau visited in the 1950s and declared it to be one of the finest diving spots in the world. Onshore, Cozumel has a relaxed atmosphere, making it the perfect spot for families.

1 Punta Santa Cecilia and Chen Río

The east side of the island is more rugged and windblown than the west, with rocky, empty beaches and crashing surf that can be dangerous to swim in. At Punta Santa Cecilia there's a quiet beach bar, Mezcalito's, which has great views, while Chen Río *(p103)* has a lovely sheltered beach and a seafood restaurant idyllically situated right on the shore.

TOP TIP

Catch great views while snorkeling or free-diving in the shallow reefs of Cozumel.

2 Laguna Chankanaab

Created around a natural coral lagoon *(p61)*, this glorious park includes a botanical garden (full of various native species), a pretty beach, and reefs that are ideal for divers of all levels, including novices.

3 North Beach Hotel Zone

The island's biggest upscale hotel cluster is situated along a shaded boulevard north of town. Hotels and resorts line a row of intimate beaches. Pools, watersports, and every comfort are on hand, and there are fine views across the channel to the Yucatán mainland from most hotel rooms.

Colorful sponges at the Palancar Reef

4 Playa Mia and Playa San Francisco

The Playa Mia and Playa San Francisco are Cozumel's best beaches, with the option to rent water tricycles and kayaks.

5 San Miguel

Cozumel's only town has a laid-back street life centered on the waterfront (Malecón) and Plaza Cozumel. The island's Punta Langosta cruise terminal is located here.

6 Paraíso Reef

Shallow and close to the shore, Paraíso Reef *(p67)* is a favorite spot for snorkeling, scuba courses, and easy diving by day and night. Parrotfish are commonly sighted.

Historic clock tower in San Miguel

7 Museo de Cozumel

Av Rafael E. Melgar 321-Planta Alta
(987) 872 0833
9am–5pm Tue–Sun

San Miguel's charming waterfront museum tells the story of Maya Cozumel, the arrival of the Spaniards, and the pirate era. It has a cozy rooftop café.

8 Palancar Reef

The most famous of Cozumel's shallow reefs, the Palancar Reef *(p67)* has fabulous coral canyons and red and blue caves. The waters are full of vibrant creatures, including the luminous angelfish.

9 San Gervasio Site

Cozumel's Maya capital, San Gervasio *(p95)* was one of the richest religious and trading cities in pre-Conquest Yucatán. The layout of its pyramids and small palaces gives a strong impression of everyday life in a Maya community.

MAYA COZUMEL

As a shrine to Ixchel, goddess of fertility, Cozumel was one of the most important places of pilgrimage in the Yucatán in the centuries just before the Spanish invasion. A visit here was seen as especially important for childless women, though everyone in Maya Yucatán tried to make the trip at least once in their lives.

10 Punta Sur Eco Beach Park

The Punta Sur Eco Beach Park *(p63)* is a diverse nature reserve with turtle-nesting beaches, huge mangroves, and lagoons that are home to crocodiles and flamingos, and a snorkeling area. There's also a lighthouse, a small Maya temple, and a maritime museum, which highlights the cultural and religious heritage of Cozumel.

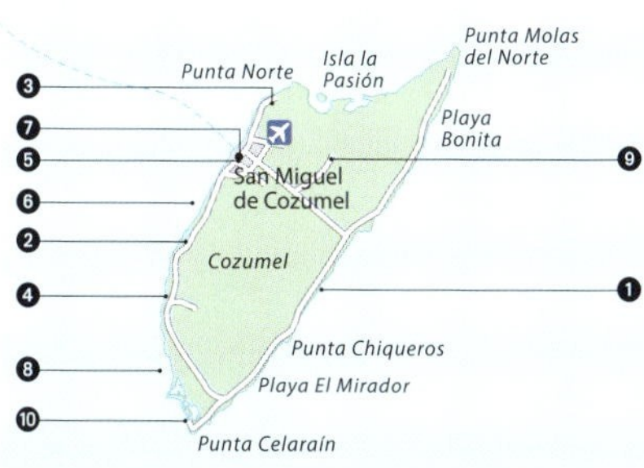

PLAYA DEL CARMEN

Q4 Av 20 and 1 Sur; mexicancaribbean.travel

Once a quiet fishing village, Playa del Carmen transformed in the early 1990s with the arrival of the first backpackers. Since then, Playa has gradually evolved into a fun spot, attracting travelers with its relaxed beach town vibe and lively nightlife.

1 Quinta Avenida

Stretching north from the town plaza, "Fifth Avenue" is Playa's main strip, for daytime shopping and nighttime promenading – a multi-colored array of shops, cafés, hotels, clubs, and restaurants.

2 Playacar

This smartly landscaped development *(p88)* shows a different side of Playa. It encompasses resort hotels, winding lanes of luxury villas, Maya sites, beach clubs, restaurants, and a championship-standard golf course.

3 Chunzubul Beach

Playa's best snorkeling spot *(p89)* is found along the beautiful Chunzubul reef, just off the beach by the same name. There are also nudist beaches along this stretch of coast.

4 INTI Beach

This spot has a more relaxed ambience than some of the area's see-and-be-seen clubs, which is precisely why many visitors love it. The club's restaurant on the beach is a top draw.

5 Town Beach

At the center of the action by day is the main beach, with beautiful soft, white Yucatán sand and plenty of shoreline cafés. Beach volleyball is something of a specialty.

6 Nighttime Playa

After dark the Quinta buzzes with crowds strolling, dining, and bar-

Clockwise from below
One of the many luxury tropical resorts in Playacar; colorful stalls lining Quinta Avenida; ruins at the Xaman-Ha Maya Site; a pair of American flamingos at Xcaret

Waves crashing on a white-sand beach at Playa del Carmen

hopping. With mariachi bands in some places and techno DJs in others, there's plenty of variety. The heart of the action is the junction of the Quinta and Calle 12.

7 Playa's Hip Hotels

Playa is well known for its stylish hotels, including the Etéreo on Paseo Kanai *(p131)*. Discreetly spectacular and with lovely pools, they showcase contemporary elegance.

PARTY ALL DAY AND ALL NIGHT

Playa del Carmen isn't known as a party hub for no reason – you really can party all night here and the fun doesn't stop, with celebrations carrying on all day long too. Establishments, including the Coralina Daylight Club *(p91)* make use of their warm and sandy locations to attract patrons while the sun is still up.

8 Museo Choco-Story

Av Constituyentes
10am–10pm daily
choco-storymexico.com

The town's Chocolate Museum features seven interactive galleries, all dedicated to one of the region's main natural products – cacao. Hands-on workshops demonstrate how it transforms from bean to bar.

9 Xaman-Ha Maya Site

Bahia del Espiritu Santo s/n, Fracc. Playacar

Playa shares its ground with an ancient Maya settlement, known as Xaman-Ha. Founded in the 13th century as part of the Ekab chiefdom during the Maya Postclassic Period, it served as a key departure point for pilgrimages to nearby temples. Today, several ruins remain, with most scattered around the Playacar area.

10 Xcaret

Created around a natural lagoon, 4 miles (6 km) south of Playa, this "eco-park" *(p87)* is teeming with flora, fauna, and sea life *(p28)*.

CALLE 46
CALLE 38
AVENIDA 30
AVENIDA 10
CALLE 26
AVE CONSTITUYENTES
CALLE 12
AVENIDA 25
AVENIDA 15
AVENIDA 5
CALLE 1
Caribbean Sea
PASEO COBA
Playacar
PASEO XAMAN-HA
10 4 miles (6 km)
3
8
1
5
4
9
2

Xcaret

1. La Caleta Cove and Blue Lagoon

Both of these are fine places in Xcaret *(p87)* for a relaxing swim. La Caleta ("the Inlet") was the main harbor of Maya Polé and is now a favorite snorkeling spot, with coral and tropical fish just below the surface. The Blue Lagoon is a big, ultra-relaxing clearwater pool behind the beach, with islands of thick vegetation to explore.

2. Hacienda Henequenera

Henequen, a fiber derived from the agave plant, was a major industry in the Yucatán during the colonial period. This 19th-century mansion takes visitors back in time to learn more about this important part of Yucatecan history.

3. Sea Trek

A fabulous guided walk – not swim – right along the seabed, using simple breathing apparatus and weights to prevent you from floating upward. You don't need to be a strong swimmer to enjoy this, and on the way you'll see all kinds of wonderful sea life from below.

4. Mariposario Butterfly Garden

One of the most spectacular parts of Xcaret, the Mariposario is the largest butterfly garden in the world. Nestled in a steep ravine beneath a giant net-like canopy, this lush garden features all kinds of exuberant tropical flowers, plants, and an astonishing variety of colorful butterfly species native to the Yucatán Peninsula. The best time to visit is in the morning when many species can be spotted.

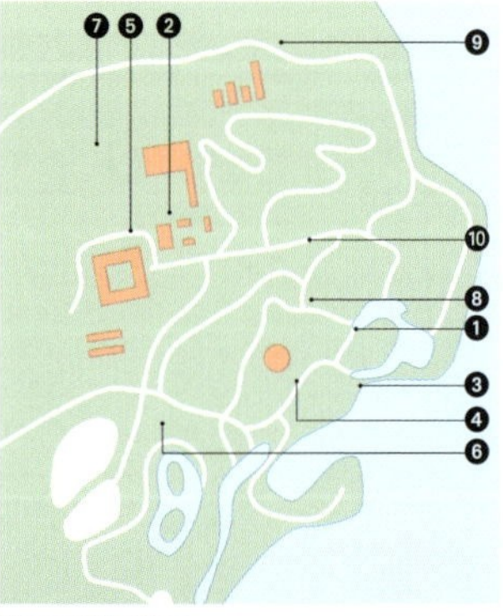

Xcaret Site Plan

A swimming and snorkeling river at Xcaret

5. Living Orchid and Bromeliad Museum

In this living museum, there are 89 of the 105 orchid species native to the region, many of which are at risk of extinction. Look out for the *Vanilla planifolia*, growing alongside the orchids.

6. Turtle Pools

Near La Caleta, you will have the chance to see different kinds of sea turtles – leatherbacks, hawksbills, and loggerheads – in every stage of life, from tiny newborns to grumpy-faced ancients with beautiful shells over 3 ft (1 m) long. The pools are part of a repopulation program to preserve this endangered species, with turtles born here being released into the sea at 15 months. Visitors must maintain a safe distance while turtle-watching.

7. Maya Village and Ball Court

Reached via a series of atmospheric passageways, the Maya Village tries to re-create some of the life of the ancient Maya world. This includes a reconstruction of a Maya ball court, where a modern interpretation of the mysterious, long-lost ball game *(p39)* is played daily. There's also a museum by the park entrance.

8. Forest Trail and Orchid Greenhouse

A well-signposted trail helps you to explore many other parts of the park, through lush natural forest and passing further attractions, such as beehives, animal enclosures, a mushroom farm, and a wonderful greenhouse with more than 100 magnificent varieties of rare orchid. You can also explore a longer, guided trail on horseback.

9. Underground Snorkeling River

This clear, winding, turquoise stream allows visitors to swim and snorkel all the way through the park and the Maya Village to the beach, via rocky canyons, pools, and caverns lit by shafts of daylight.

10. Live Show

Presented nightly, this is a spectacular mix of entertainment spread all around the village and theater. It begins with "ancient Maya" rituals, mariachis, and vibrant performances of folk music and dances from all over Mexico, and goes on to a *charrería*, or Mexican rodeo.

Live show depicting ancient Maya rituals

ISLA MUJERES

L1–2 Av Rueda Medina 130; caribemexicano.travel

The beautiful Isla Mujeres ("Island of Women"), 12 miles (20 km) east of Cancún, got its name from Ixchel, the Maya goddess of fertility, who revered the island. Despite its proximity to Cancún, the island offers a relaxed atmosphere and is a favorite among backpackers, with excellent diving and fishing opportunities.

1 Isla Town

Isla's only town retains the charm of a Caribbean fishing village, with its narrow, sandy streets and wooden houses. It is home to plenty of cafés and souvenir shops.

2 Parque Garrafón

This nature park *(p60)* and snorkeling center is created around a natural, shallow pool. Relax in the restaurants or go swimming or snorkeling in the swimming pools and rock pools. Divers can rent equipment and head to the offshore reefs.

3 Guadalupe Chapel

Av Perimetral Oriente (998) 705 9911 For mass: 8am Sun

A humble yet beautiful church, the Guadalupe Chapel looks out onto the sea and offers a truly inspiring view. There's a small gift shop on site, which sells handmade jewelry. The chapel also serves as a venue for events such as *quinceañeras* (a young girl's coming-of-age celebration) and weddings.

4 Playa Norte

This beach *(p89)*, at the northern tip of the town, is where many Isla visitors spend their days, with soft white sand and laid-back beach bars for refreshment breaks. The calm

TOP TIP

Ultramar ferries *(p125)* offers affordable services with daily departures to the island.

turquoise waters mean it's also excellent for a relaxing swim.

5 Playa Secreto To the northeast of Isla town, this "secret" beach *(p89)* is in a sheltered inlet that's even more shallow and placid than Playa Norte.

6 Manchones Reef This is Isla Mujeres' favorite reef *(p67)* for scuba courses and easy diving. Only about 30–40 ft (10–12 m) deep, the waters are safe and have plenty of colorful coral and fish to observe.

7 Parque Escultórico Punta Sur
10am–6pm daily
The southern tip of the island has been transformed into a sculpture park with striking modern artworks spread around the windblown headland and lighthouse.

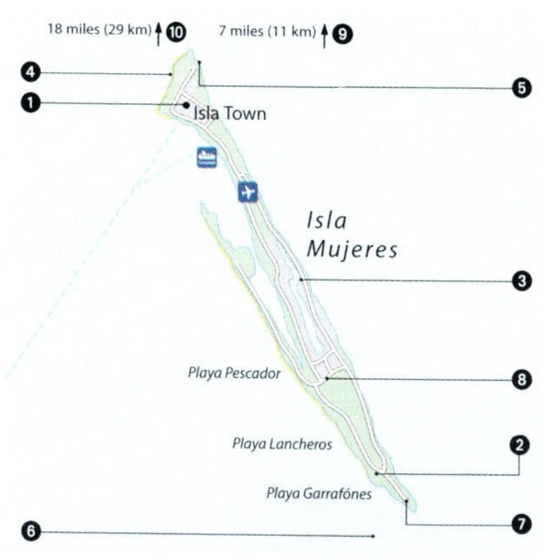

8 Women's Beading Cooperative
La Gloria s/n Manzana, 160 Lote
9am–5pm Mon–Sat, 10am–2pm Sun
Nearly 60 women are working members of this cooperative and earn a living by making jewelry. Visitors are welcome.

9 Sleeping Sharks Cave
An underground river meets the sea here, and sharks come to bask, trancelike, in the mixture of fresh and salt water. A must-see for experienced divers; keep a safe distance from the sharks.

10 Isla Contoy An uninhabited island about 18 miles (29 km) north of Isla Mujeres, Contoy *(p62)* is a important seabird reserve. Day trips are run by companies on Isla.

Turquoise waters of Parque Garrafón

THE LAFITTES

Isla's Mujeres' most famous residents were the 19th-century Louisiana-born brothers Jean and Pierre Lafitte, considered the last infamous Caribbean pirates. Sailing south after falling out with the US government, they built a stronghold on the Isla lagoon, but were attacked by the Spanish Navy in 1821. Both badly wounded, they escaped in a boat. Pierre is thought to have died in Dzilam Bravo on the mainland; Jean's fate remains a mystery.

TULUM

P6 visittulum.travel

One of the Yucatán's most beautiful places, Tulum offers visitors a breathtaking mix of ancient Maya ruins and miles of superb, palm-fringed beaches. Known for its cabañas – simple, palm-roofed cabins set right by the beach – Tulum also has a vibrant culinary scene with a variety of dining and drinking spots.

Freediver at the entrance to a cenote

1 Tulum Maya Site

8am–5pm daily
inah.gob.mx
Maya Tulum was a walled town and prosperous trading community when the Spaniards arrived in the 1520s. This site includes a recognizable main street, the House of the Columns, and the Palace of the Halach Uinic.

TOP TIP

In peak season the cheaper beach cabañas are often booked up by 10am.

2 Tulum Pueblo

A rambling place spread out along the main highway, Tulum village was almost 100 percent Maya, but it now has a bank, bus terminus, cafés, small hotels, and backpacker services for visitors.

3 Playa Paraíso

Set against a backdrop of the iconic El Castillo, Paradise Beach is widely considered one of the best beaches in Mexico. It has clean sand and clear Caribbean waters, and is a must-visit for visitors to Tulum.

4 Secluded Heaven

Along a stretch of beach south of the T-junction in the road is a wide choice of beach cabins, from sand-floor huts to luxurious cabañas, most of them secluded. Few have electricity so most are lit only by candles at night.

El Castillo temple overlooking the sea

5 Xel-Ha

This coral inlet *(p96)* has been landscaped as a snorkel park with plenty of colorful fish. It also has a forest trail and beach, and is great for families. Across the highway is the site of a Maya city.

6 Gran Cenote

Along the road toward Cobá from Tulum are several accessible cenotes in which visitors can take a cooling dip. One of the area's best options for swimming

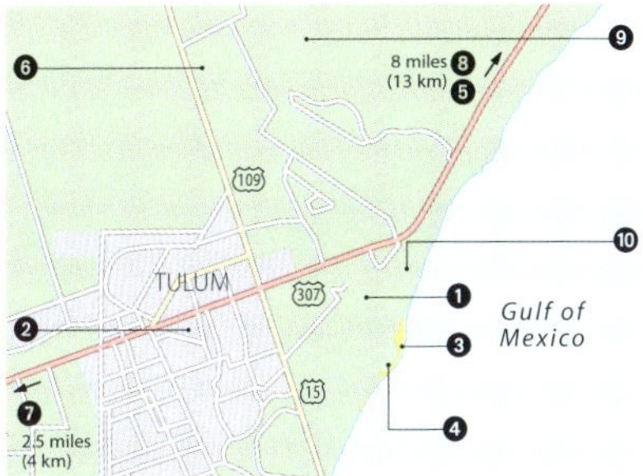

and snorkeling is the Gran Cenote *(p98)*. A path of beautiful wildflowers leads into a wide, arching cavern, all surrounded by imposing rock columns.

7 Aktun-Ha Cenote

An enjoyable cenote *(p98)* for swimming, with a broad, peaceful pool that runs into a dark and mysterious cave system. While swimming, you'll spot shoals of tiny fish.

8 Dos Ojos Cenote

This is the entrance to one of the longest known underwater cave systems *(p99)*, which stretches over 220 miles (350 km).

9 Tankah Natural Park

9am–5pm Mon–Sat
tankah.com.mx

Located west of Tankah Bay, the park offers jeep, zip-line, and canoe rides through lush forests, as well as the opportunity to visit a Maya village located within the park.

10 El Castillo

9am–5pm daily
tulumruins.net

The most impressive local Maya building is this temple. A flaming beacon at the top of the temple was once visible for miles.

CENOTES

Some 65 million years ago an asteroid struck the Yucatán. The impact formed vast networks of lime stone caves, sub terranean rivers, and cenotes, natural sinkholes fed by springs. Some cenotes are open for diving or swimming, which is a great experience.

SIAN KA'AN BIOSPHERE RESERVE

F4–G6 Quintana Roo 7am–6pm daily

The jungle and wetlands of Sian Ka'an (Mayan for "where the sky is born") contrast strikingly with the resorts of the Riviera Maya. Extending south from Tulum around Ascension Bay and encompassing lagoons, reefs, lakes, mangroves, and forests, the area is virtually uninhabited and contains a dazzling variety of animal and plant life.

1 Muyil Site

The Maya city of Muyil *(p99)* lies just outside the reserve. An ancient city allied to Cobá *(p96)*, it has an unusual pyramid with a large multiroomed building at its top. Beside the site, a path leads to Lake Chunyaxché.

2 Lake Chunyaxché

G4

Sian Ka'an has many lakes fed by underground streams. The channels from *Laguna Campechén* into Lake Chunyaxché and have points where the sea and lake meet, bringing together a mix of plant life and fish.

3 Ben-Ha Cenote

G4

By the warden's lodge at the reserve's entrance, a path leads to a clear, cool cenote, where you can swim among reeds and forest trees.

TOP TIP

If you're traveling without a guide, be sure to eat or stock up on food at Punta Allen.

4 Boca Paila

G4

Boca Paila is a glorious lagoon that's a magnet for serious fishers. It's also where Sian Ka'an tours switch from vans to boats.

5 Punta Allen

It is said that this lobster-fishing village, *(p68)* with its sandy streets, big beach, and

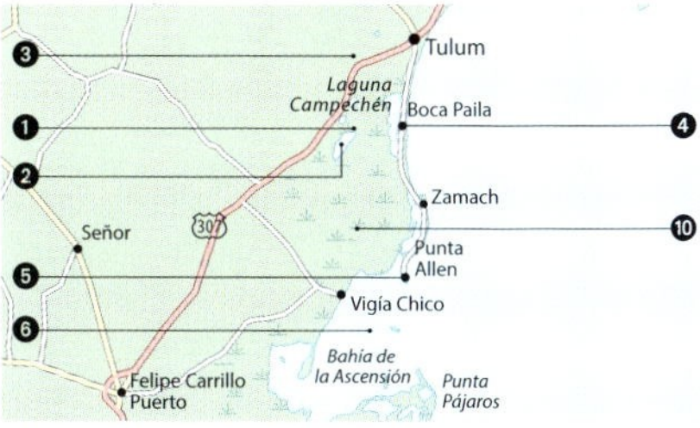

Scenic Sian Ka'an Biosphere Reserve

CHECHEN AND CHAKAH

Also known as black poisonwood, the chechen tree is highly toxic. Its aroma alone can make people numb and dizzy. But if local Maya ever come into contact with the tree's leaves, they know to search for a chakah bush, which provides the antidote to the chechen's poison.

handful of places to eat and stay, was founded by Blackbeard, whose ship was called *The Allen*.

6 Ascension Bay Bonefishing Flats

G5

These shallows are among the best fly-fishing areas in the world, above all for bonefish. Lodges along the road, and Punta Allen's guesthouses, offer trips to them.

7 Lake Islands

There are more than 20 Maya sites within the reserve, many of them are small temples situated on islands in the lakes. It is thought that these isolated lake-island temples were likely pilgrimage sites, visited by worshipers to perform special rituals.

8 Animals

Sian Ka'an is home to every kind of wild cat found in Mexico and Central America, including ocelots and pumas, as well as other wild animals such as anteaters, manatees, and tapirs. However, the most common ones that you're most likely to see are raccoons, spider monkeys, bush pigs, iguanas, and gray foxes.

9 Native and Migratory Birds

Nearly 350 bird species have been logged as native to the Sian Ka'an Biosphere Reserve, and around a million migratory birds visit each year from North America. Among those easiest for visitors to see are ibises, egrets, orioles, storks, American herons, and flamingos.

10 Mangroves and Forest

A mix of salt- and freshwater at Sian Ka'an Biosphere Reserve provides the ideal conditions for the growth of mangroves. Farther inland there are vast expanses of verdant rainforest and grasslands.

Frigate birds atop a mangrove tree

CHICHÉN ITZÁ

E3 · 8am–4pm daily · chichenitza.com

Built on a grand scale, Chichén Itzá, one of the seven wonders of the world, has some of the largest buildings of the ancient Maya cities. It had a port near Río Lagartos and grew rich from trading. With a large population, it became the most powerful city in the whole of the Yucatán in the last centuries of the Classical Maya era (around 750–900 CE), defeating Cobá, Izamal, and others.

1 Observatory

The observatory is also called El Caracol ("snail") for its odd round shape. Three slots in its top level point due south and toward the setting sun and moon on the spring and fall equinoxes.

2 Nunnery

The Spaniards thought this group of buildings was a nunnery, but experts now believe it formed the main residential and administrative area for Chichén Itzá's lords in the city's first years. The buildings are covered in a wealth of spectacular carvings.

3 Great Ball Court

Built in 864 CE, this is the biggest ancient ball court *(p39)* in Mexico. It has exceptional carvings and remarkably good acoustics.

TOP TIP

To beat the large groups that arrive around 11am, stay nearby the night before.

4 Castillo de Kukulcán

It is no longer possible to climb this awesome pyramid, which encloses an older one that is accessed from the top of the Castillo. The marvelous carvings, panels, levels, and the 365 steps are symbols of the intricate Maya calendar.

People swimming in the giant Sacred Cenote

5 Temple of the Warriors

The squat temple opposite the Castillo was used in city rituals. In front of it are ranks of pillars, each intricately carved with portraits of important figures in the Chichén Itzá elite.

6 High Priest's Grave

This pyramid is inscribed with the date of its completion: June 20, 842. It is named for a tomb excavated at its foot, which cannot be visited.

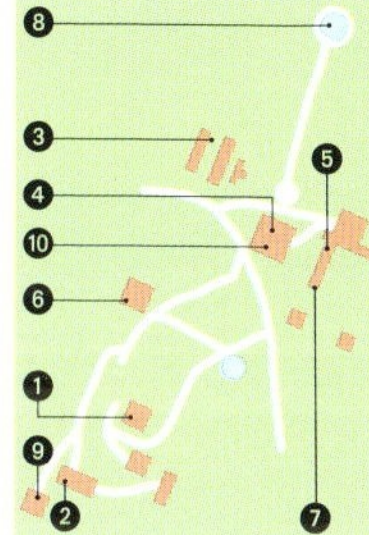

Chichén Itzá Site Plan

7 Court of the Thousand Columns

The forest of pillars around a giant quadrangle once supported wood and palm roofs. This was Chichén's main place for doing business: buying, selling, and voicing disputes.

8 Sacred Cenote

Visited by Maya pilgrims over many centuries, the Sacred Cenote is a giant natural sinkhole *(p64)*. This mysterious cenote has yielded up jewelry, sculptures, and bones of animals.

9 Old Chichén

Chichén Itzá once covered a much wider area than is seen at its monumental core today. To the south is Chichén Viejo – a partially excavated site in the woods that is as old as the central plazas.

10 Sound and Light Show

From 7pm daily
nochesdekukulkan.com.mx

Presented nightly, this show features an imagined history of Chichén Itzá, while the main temples are dramatically lit.

Impressive Castillo de Kukulcán

EQUINOX "DESCENT"

On the spring equinox, the afternoon sun picks out the tails of the serpents lining the Castillo's north stairway and runs down to their heads just before sunset. On the fall equinox, the reverse effect occurs. This "Descent of Kukulcán" symbolized the city's contact with the gods. Today, crowds flock to see the event.

The Carvings

Chac-Masks of Las Monjas on the Nunnery's facade

1. Chac-Masks of Las Monjas

The curling snout of Chac, the god of rain and lightning, is depicted repeatedly in rows at the Nunnery.

2. Casa Colorada Inscriptions

These record that Chichén Itzá's lords celebrated a ritual in September 869 CE to ensure the city's prosperity.

3. Platform of the Jaguars and Eagles

This small platform may have been used for rituals by the warrior Orders of the Jaguars and Eagles. Its carvings show these animals tearing open human victims to eat their hearts.

4. Chac Mool and Altar of the Red Jaguar

Reclining Chac Mool figures were fallen warriors delivering offerings to the gods, ranging from food and jewels to even the hearts of sacrificial victims. The Chac Mool in the temple of the Castillo lies before a painted stone jaguar throne.

5. Temple of the Jaguars

Carved panels in this temple connect the foundation of Chichén Itzá with First Mother and First Father, the creators of the world.

6. Ball Court Frieze

As defeated ball game players have their heads cut off, seven spurts of blood shoot from their necks and transform into vines and flowers.

7. Heads of Kukulcán

The giant feathered serpents at the Castillo probably represented Vision Serpents but they have also been associated with the central Mexican serpent-god Quetzalcóatl.

8. Tzompantli

Covered in carved skulls, a low platform near the Ball Court was probably used to display the heads of sacrificial victims.

9. Warriors' Columns

A "picture gallery" of the men of Chichén Itzá. Most are of warriors in their battle regalia, but there are also some priests and bound captives.

10. Snails, Armadillos, Turtles, and Crabs

Placed between the Chac-heads on the Iglesia ("church"), these animals represented the four spirits that held up the sky at the cardinal points (north, south, east, west) in Maya mythology.

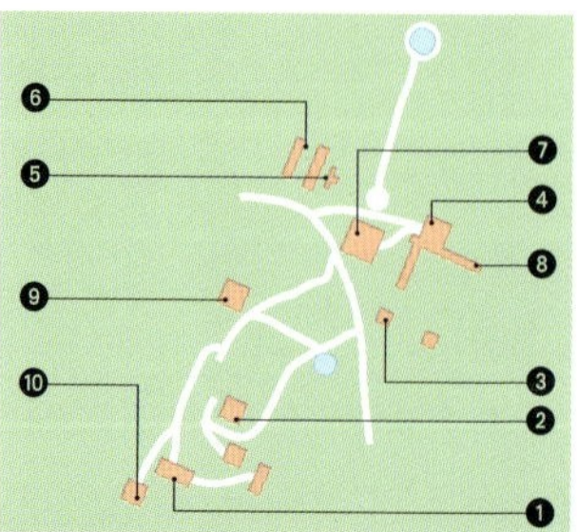

Chichén Itzá Site Plan

TOP 10
ANCIENT MAYA
BALL COURTS

1. Monte Albán, Oaxaca
2. Palenque, Chiapas
3. Toniná, Chiapas
4. Uxmal, Yucatán
5. Chichén Itzá, Yucatán
6. Cobá, Quintana Roo
7. Kohunlich, Quintana Roo
8. Calakmul, Campeche
9. Tikal, Guatemala
10. Copán, Honduras

THE BALL GAME

Intricately carved stone ball-hoop

This ancient Mexican ball game can be traced back to before 1500 BCE. It features in Maya myths such as the story of the hero-twins Hunahpu and Xbalanqué, who play the game with the Lords of Death for days and nights, defying the forces of destiny. The game was played in ball courts that were usually I-shaped as depicted in Aztec codex illustrations. No one knows exactly how the game was played, but it is thought that there were two main forms. One was played by two or four players on the older, smaller courts, and the aim was to keep the ball from touching the ground and get it past your opponent(s) and out at the end of the court. The other form corresponded to much bigger courts, such as at Chichén Itzá, and was played by teams of seven who scored in big rings on either side of the court. In either style, players could not touch the ball with hands or feet, but only with shoulders, chest, and hips, so scoring was very hard. Games had great ritual significance, symbolizing the cycle of life, with the court itself representing the world. It is believed that bets were placed on the results and sometimes, but not always, losing players were sacrificed to the gods.

Illustration of a Maya ball court and the ball-game players in action

MÉRIDA

C2 Palacio Municipal, Calle 56A, 242; merida.gob.mx/capitalcultural

Once Mexico's wealthiest city due to its booming henequen industry – an agave fiber popularly known as "green gold" – Mérida still showcases many vestiges of its storied past, most notably in its grand homes, public buildings, and lively plazas. As Yucatán's capital, it's the perfect place to learn about the region's rich culture.

1 Cathedral

Also widely known as the Catedral de San Ildefonso, this landmark *(p53)* was built between 1562 and 1598. It is the oldest cathedral on the American mainland (in the entire continent, only Santo Domingo in the Dominican Republic is older). Massive and monumental, the cathedral was built in the style of the Spanish Renaissance, with a soaring facade and relatively few decorative flourishes.

2 Palacio del Gobernador

Calle 59, 535
8am–9pm daily

Situated next to the cathedral, the elegant seat of the Yucatán state government was built in 1892 to replace a Spanish governors' palace. Its patios feature striking murals by Mexican artist Fernando Castro Pacheco, depicting the Maya story. There's also a museum showcasing the interesting regional artwork.

3 Iglesia de Jesús

The Jesuits built this church *(p53)* in 1618, favoring ornamentation and flair over the plain style of the Franciscans, who built most of the city's religious buildings.

4 Paseo de Montejo

Laid out in the Yucatán's early 1900s boom in the style of Parisian boulevards, this avenue is lined with magnificent mansions, some using Maya iconography.

Exploring the Plaza Mayor

5 Market

One of the Yucatán's main shopping hubs, this market *(p119)* features stalls with products such as food, hammocks, sandals, *jipijapa* straw hats, and embroidered goods.

6 Parque Santa Lucía

The arcaded square of Santa Lucía, dating in part from 1575, is the most romantic of all Mérida's old squares. Free concerts of traditional music take place here every Thursday.

7 Museo Casa Montejo

Palacio de Montejo, Calle 63, 506 10am–6pm Tue–Sun (to 2pm Sun)

Mérida's first Spanish stone house has a stunning portico completed in 1549, with a depiction of the Conquest.

8 Museo de Antropología

Palacio Cantón, Calle 43, 485 8am–5pm Tue–Sun inah.gob.mx

One of Mexico's most important archaeological museums is set in the grandest of all the Paseo Montejo mansions, built for General Francisco Cantón between 1909 and 1911. The museum has many treasures that have been excavated from sites across the Yucatán, and is especially rich in ceramics and jade. It offers an overview of the Maya world that illuminates visits to the sites.

9 Gran Museo del Mundo Maya

Calle 60 Norte, 299 E 9am–5pm Wed–Mon granmuseodelmundomaya.com.mx

This museum has a fascinating array of exhibits from the Maya world, ranging from religious artifacts to daily life tools. There's a sound-and-light show held on Fridays and weekends.

10 Plaza Mayor

This spacious square was the heart of the historic Maya city of Ti'ho, and was made the new city's hub by conquistador Francisco Montejo, when he founded Mérida in 1542. It is surrounded by the city's main public buildings, while its lovely colonnades and benches, set under giant laurel trees, provide favorite meeting places. Visitors often come here to stroll and relax.

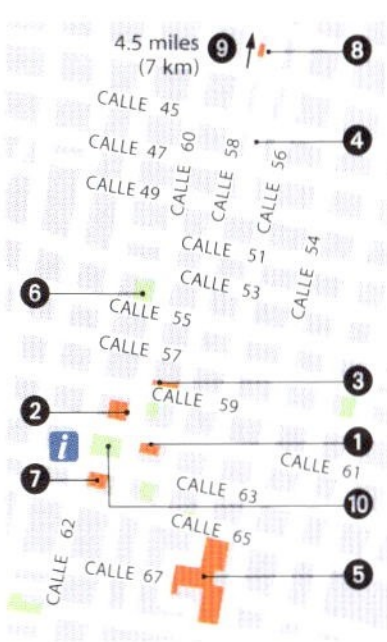

THE TRÍOS

Stroll through Plaza Mayor on most evenings and you'll spot groups of men in threes, dressed in white shirts and black trousers, carrying guitars. These are the Yucatán *tríos*, traditional troubadours for hire who perform romantic serenades. Locals often book them for parties or weddings, while others pay to hear them sing in town squares.

Exhibits at the Gran Museo del Mundo Maya

UXMAL

C4 8am–5pm daily inah.gob.mx

The most majestic and enduring of the Maya cities, Uxmal (which means "three-times-built") was a powerful city state from 700 CE to 900 CE. It was a key member of the Mayapán confederation before its decline around 1450. With grand structures that resemble gigantic stage sets, its buildings have been compared to the famous monuments of Greece and Rome.

1 Great Pyramid

Many parts of this pyramid are older than the Governor's Palace next door. Like many Maya buildings, it was altered and added to many times but is now in poor condition.

2 Pyramid of the Magician

Unusually, Uxmal's best-known pyramid has rounded corners. The temple at the top is the home of the Dwarf of Uxmal. Climbing to the top is no longer permitted.

3 House of the Pigeons

This splendid complex consists of temples and palatial residences, once covered in sculptures. Early travelers thought the lofty roof comb above its central quadrangle looked like dovecotes, hence the name.

TOP TIP

Arrive at the site early to avoid the heat and the crowds.

4 Temple of the Centipede and the Arch

Uxmal's unexcavated areas include the Temple of the Centipede. A *sacbé* (Maya road), once linked the city to its ally Kabah with an arch marking the edge of Uxmal's center.

5 Nunnery Quadrangle

This elegant complex of four buildings was at the

Admiring the intricate Nunnery Quadrangle

heart of Uxmal's power and ritual. It was so named by a Spanish friar merely because its structure reminded him of a convent. Its facade's intricate carvings *(p44)* symbolize the magical authority of the city and its rulers and their contact with the gods.

6 House of the Old Woman

Only partly excavated, this large pyramid with a Puuc-style temple on one side is among the oldest major structures at Uxmal, dating from about 700 CE. In Maya legend, it is said to be the home of the Sprite's Mother.

Iconic Pyramid of the Magician

7 House of the Turtles

This small, delicately proportioned temple-residence is considered the archetype of the pure Puuc architectural style *(p45)*. The name comes from its decorative cornice, featuring a line of turtles carved in stone. This is a motif that is seen many times at Uxmal; it was associated with the rebirth of new life and the fertility of the coming of the rains.

8 Ball Court

Uxmal's main ball court is smaller than the Great Court at Chichén Itzá *(p39)*. The original scoring rings are inscribed with dates from the year 901; those you see at the court are replicas.

9 Governor's Palace

Often regarded as the finest of all Maya buildings, this huge palace, over 300 ft (91 m) long, was built for the greatest of Uxmal's rulers, known as Chan-Chak-Kaknal-Ahaw, or Lord Chak. Its huge frieze symbolizes the passage of time as well as the cycles of rain, sun, and rebirth.

UXMAL'S SPRITE

In Maya legend, Uxmal was founded by an *alux* (Sprite), who had defied the authority of a local king. When the king dared the sprite to build a house, the Pyramid of the Magician appeared overnight. On another day, the sprite built the path to Kabah. The king's last test was that they should both be hit on the head with hammers. The king died, but the sprite was protected by a magic tortilla and went on to rule Uxmal.

10 Sound-and-Light Show

Winter: 7pm daily, summer: 8pm daily
nochesdekukulkan.com.mx

Every night, Uxmal's major buildings are dramatically lit up in varying colors, with a commentary on the city's history and legends.

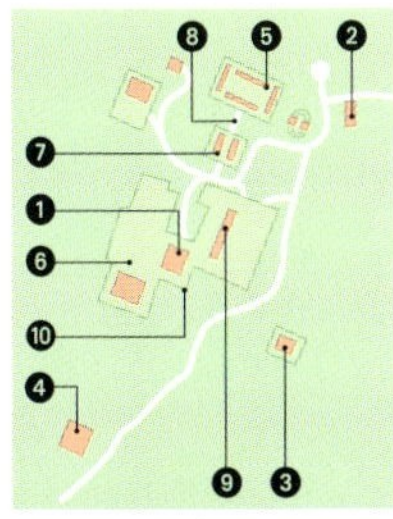

Uxmal Site Plan

The Carvings

Carved stone bas-reliefs of Vision Serpents

1. Nunnery: Vision Serpents
The patterns on the East Building are Vision Serpents, conduits between men and the "Otherworld."

2. Monstermouths
Temple entrances in the form of giant faces, such as on the House of the Dwarf at the Pyramid of the Magician, made a striking connection between the temple and the gods of the earth.

3. Nunnery: Serpent Heads
The huge feathered snakes winding around the West Building are probably Vision Serpents. Human faces emerge from their jaws.

4. Nunnery Quadrangle: Maya Huts
A distinctive feature of Puuc carving is the combination of complex symbols with everyday images. The huts carved on the South Building of the Nunnery are very little different from those seen in Yucatecan villages today.

5. Parrots of the Great Pyramid
Stylized *guaca-mayas* (macaws) feature prominently as symbols of uncontrolled nature in the carvings on the temple at the top of the Great Pyramid.

6. Nunnery: Flowers and Lattices
Latticework represented the huts in which meetings were held, while flowers symbolized magic. The combination of the two denoted a ceremonial site.

7. Muyal Symbols
The simple spiral pattern seen frequently on the Nunnery and Governor's Palace represents the Mayan word for cloud, *muyal*, yet another symbol of contact with the heavens.

8. Lord Chak
The figure in a spectacular headdress set within the facade of the Governor's Palace is believed to be the legendary Lord Chak himself.

9. La Picota
The phallic column called the "whipping-post" in Spanish has inscriptions on it that have never been deciphered. It formed part of a fertility cult that was a distinctive feature of Uxmal.

10. Birds Quadrangle
This courtyard, bounded by four large structures, was given its name because of the beautiful images of macaws and other birds intricately carved on the west building.

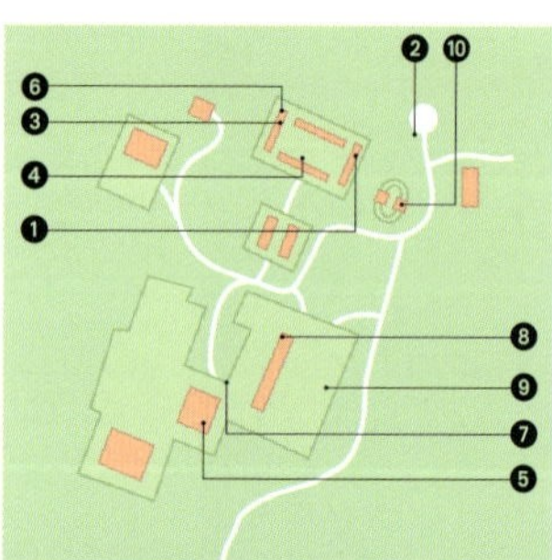

Uxmal Site Plan

THE PUUC CITIES

TOP 10
PUUC CITIES

1. Oxkintok
2. Uxmal
3. Kabah
4. Sayil
5. Nohpat
6. Xlapak
7. Labná
8. Chacmultún
9. Xcalumkín
10. Itzimté

Carved building stones at Kabah

Uxmal was the largest of a string of Maya communities that flourished in the Puuc Hills of southern Yucatán around 650–920 CE. The other well-known cities are Kabah, Sayil, Xlapak, and Labná *(p115)*. Their distinctive style of architecture is the most refined of those used by Maya builders, and is characterized by strong horizontal lines, elegant proportions, and a sharp contrast between plain lower walls and rows of elaborately carved friezes above them. Many architectural details seem to mimic humbler buildings and natural features, such as the small drum columns along the bottom of many Puuc walls, which imitate the stick walls of village huts. Some buildings, such as the Codz Poop (Palace of Masks) at Kabah are decorated with images of gods. The communities that lived in these cities were wealthy but fragile, because this region is one of the driest parts of the Yucatán. Indeed, severe drought was probably a major reason why the southern Maya cities collapsed in 800–950 CE. A one- or two-day tour of the main Puuc cities is possible, following the Puuc Route, south of Uxmal.

Exquisite stone lattice-work at Kabah

10

CAMPECHE

A5 Av Ruíz Cortines; (981) 127 3300

The colonial city of Campeche, built in the 16th century, was once a trading stronghold of the Spanish empire. Today, it's a remarkable museum piece with its cobbled streets and colorful houses that still sit within the historic city walls, built to fend off pirate attacks. The city's main museum displays Maya relics from the excavated forest city of Calakmul.

1 Palacio Centro Cultural

Housed in an attractive building on the Parque Principal, this museum *(p79)* charts the history of the city through multimedia displays, a sound-and-light show, and exhibits that include a replica Spanish galleon.

2 Museo de las Estelas Mayas

Puerta de Mar
8am–5pm Tue–Sun

After the city walls were built, Puerta de Mar provided a gateway to the harbor. This bastion now houses the Museo de las Estelas Mayas, which displays carvings from sites around Campeche.

3 Casa Seis

Calle 57, No. 6, Zona Centro

A gracious old house, this casa has been restored to re-create the home of a prosperous

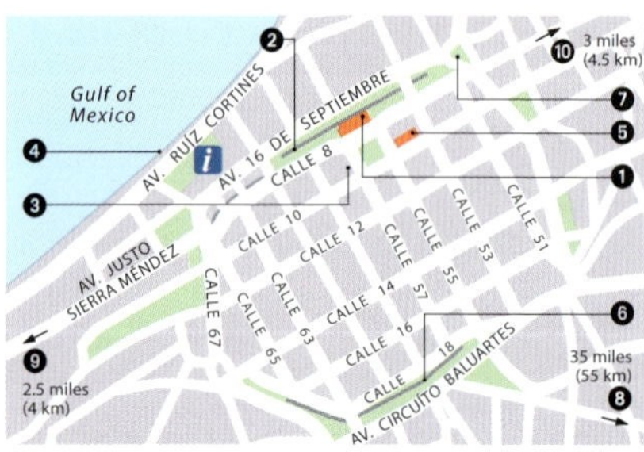

Colorful buildings lining a street

19th-century Campeche merchant. The house's patio hosts a tourist information desk and also features concerts and exhibitions.

4 The Malecón

This waterfront has been restored and is a popular place for locals to take a stroll. There are often superb sunsets over the Gulf of Mexico.

5 Cathedral

Begun in the 1560s, the cathedral *(p53)* in Campeche was not completed until the 19th century. Its facade is one of the oldest parts, designed in a Spanish Renaissance style typical of many churches built in the reign of King Philip II.

6 Puerta de Tierra

Calle 59 and Calle 18 9am–8pm daily

Built in 1732, the Puerta de Tierra ("Land Gate") was the only way in or out of Campeche on the landward side. Within is a museum of maritime and pirate history.

7 Baluarte de Santiago

Av 16 de Septiembre and Calle 49

This isolated bastion has been imaginatively used to house a dense and verdant botanical garden, with giant palms and other tropical flora.

8 Edzná

This city *(p118)*, 35 miles (55 km) southeast of Campeche, once rivaled Chichén Itzá and Uxmal in size and wealth. Its palace-temple, known as the "Building of the Five Stories," is one of the largest, most intricate Maya buildings.

9 Fuerte San Miguel Museum

Carr. Escénica, Zona Centro 8am–5pm Tue–Sun

A hilltop fortress just south of the city, this is now home to a fine collection of Maya relics, including a set of beautiful jade funeral masks.

10 Fuerte San José Museum

Av Francisco Morazán 8am–5pm Tue–Sun

This sturdy Spanish fortress houses the Post-Conquest sections of the town's popular museum. There are lovely sea and city views that can be seen easily from the ramparts.

THE PIRATE PLAGUE

Between the 1560s and the 1680s, Campeche was attacked again and again by pirates such as Henry Morgan and the Dutchman known only as "Peg-Leg." Finally, the Spanish governors and city's merchants had suffered enough and ordered the building of a solid ring of walls and bastions. This transformed the city into one of the largest walled cities in Spanish America. In 1999, Campeche was designated a UNESCO World Heritage Site for its well-preserved fortifications.

Mask, Fuerte San José Museum

TOP 10 OF EVERYTHING

Maya pyramids at the Ek-Balam site

POPULAR MAYA SITES

Ancient arch doorway in the Maya city of Labná

1 Labná

Set in a wooded valley full of colorful flora and fauna, Labná *(p115)* is one of the most beautiful Maya sites. It preserves a strong impression of the life that once flourished here, with its impressive buildings – most notably, the iconic Arch of Labná.

2 Kabah

Kabah *(p116)* was among the most important Puuc sites *(p45)*, after Uxmal, to which it was linked by a *sacbé* or Maya road. A grand arch at the end of this road forms a pair with the one at Uxmal *(p42)*. The area was first settled thousands of years ago, in the early Maya period, but most of the existing structures today date from the 7th–11th centuries.

3 Dzibilchaltún

Located just north of Mérida, this site *(p116)* was occupied for over 2,000 years. At dawn on spring and summer equinoxes, the sun strikes straight through the open doorways of the Temple of the Seven Dolls and along a road. There's also a great swimming cenote located here.

4 Ek-Balam

The compact city of Ek-Balam *(p108)* was little known until 1998, when excavations of its largest temple-mound revealed spectacular carvings, especially at El Trono ("The Throne"), the largest and most extravagant of Maya monster mouth temples. Other unique buildings include La Redonda, an almost spiral-shaped tower whose distinctive design remains a mystery to this day.

5 Sayil

With around 17,000 inhabitants in 850 CE, Sayil *(p116)* was among the wealthiest of the Puuc cities. This is reflected in its magnificent Palacio as well as other impressive buildings such as the Mirador Pyramid, which once stood at the center of the city's bustling market area.

6 Tulum

A small city from the last decades of Maya civilization, Tulum *(p32)* is a spectacular site as it is the only known Maya city built on cliffs overlooking the sea. It's the perfect spot to enjoy the Yucatán's stunning coastline, and learn about the region's rich cultural history.

Temple overlooking the beach and sea at Tulum

7 Chichén Itzá

The most dramatic of the Maya cities, Chichén Itzá *(p36)* has gigantic buildings, including the great Castillo de Kukulcán pyramid that has become an enduring symbol of the Yucatán.

8 Edzná

One of the largest and wealthiest cities of Classic-era Yucatán, Edzná *(p118)* features a huge palace known as the "Building of the Five Stories," which is the largest and most complex of all Maya multistory buildings.

9 Uxmal

A hugely atmospheric city, Uxmal *(p42)* has some of the finest Maya buildings in the Nunnery Quadrangle and the Governor's Palace.

10 Cobá

Before the rise of Chichén Itzá, Cobá *(p96)* was the largest city in northern Yucatán. Its buildings are spread across a huge area of forest and lakes, with the city itself situated between two lagoons, Lake Cobá and Lake Macanxoc. The city features a network of stone and plaster roads, known as *sacbé*, (white roads), which radiate outward from the central site. Some of the highlights include the Nohoch Mul, which, at 138 ft (42 m), is the highest pyramid in the Yucatán.

TOP 10 LESSER-KNOWN MAYA SITES

Stone columns at Aké

1. Aké
Built of massive columns and huge stone slabs, the city of Aké *(p107)* is unlike anywhere else in the Yucatán.

2. El Meco, Cancún
This was one of the most important city *(p88)* in pre-Hispanic times.

3. San Gervasio, Cozumel
Capital of the island when it *(p95)* was one of the great pilgrimage centers of Maya Yucatán.

4. Xel-Ha
One of the oldest Maya sites *(p98)* near the modern Riviera, with ancient murals of birds.

5. Muyil
An ancient Maya site *(p99)* next to the Sian Ka'an reserve.

6. El Rey, Cancún
The relics *(p88)* of the historic occupiers of Cancún Island can be found here.

7. Xcambó
A tiny site *(p110)* with a Catholic chapel built onto one of its pyramids.

8. Oxkintok
Oxkintok is an ancient city *(p118)* just west of the Puuc area. It rivaled Uxmal in size, and has a unique temple complex.

9. Xlapak
The Palacio has a frieze of elaborately carved Chac-masks *(p118)*.

10. Mayapán
The last major Maya city *(p118)*, which dominated the Yucatán from 1200 to 1400.

Franciscan interior of San Bernardino de Siena

CHURCHES

1 San Bernardino de Siena, Valladolid

E3

The oldest permanent church in the Yucatán began as part of a Franciscan monastery in 1552. It was located outside Valladolid *(p108)* in order to function both as a place of worship for the Spanish townsfolk and as a mission for Maya villagers. Inside is a spectacularly painted Baroque altarpiece. The cloister surrounds an overgrown, palm-filled garden with a massive stone well from 1613, built over a cenote.

2 Tekax Church

C4

Completed in 1692, this huge yet finely proportioned church was built in a lighter style than those of the early colonial period. The churches at Teabo and Oxkutzcab *(p54)* are similar.

3 San Antonio de Padua, Izamal

D2

The Izamal monastery, painted ocher and white like the rest of the city *(p108)*, epitomizes the plain, austere style favored by the Franciscan friars, who brought Catholicism to the Yucatán. It was founded in 1549, and its huge *atrio*, or courtyard, was designed to hold great crowds of Mayas worshiping in open-air masses.

4 Maní Monastery

C4

The first of all the Franciscan missionary monasteries in the Yucatán, consecrated in 1549, Maní was built very simply, with a massive stone facade and cavernous cloister. Set within the facade was an external altar or "Indian Chapel," so that open-air services could be held. In 1562, the friars infamously burned Mayan manuscripts and relics.

Richly detailed palanquin in the Maní Monastery

5 San Roque, Campeche

A5

San Roque is an extravagant example of Mexican Baroque, with a beautifully restored opulent altarpiece that is surrounded by white plasterwork.

6 La Mejorada, Mérida

C2

This large church with a very Spanish-looking plain facade was built as part of a major Franciscan friary in 1640. It was the last occupied monastery in Mérida, and closed only in 1857.

7 Las Monjas, Mérida

C2

The church of "The Nuns" was built in the 1590s as a chapel for one of the first closed convents in the Americas. The castle-like mirador, or watchtower, with its unusual loggia (covered balcony), was designed to allow the nuns to enjoy the fresh air without having to leave the convent.

8 Iglesia de Jesús, Mérida

C2

Built for the Jesuit Order and completed in 1618, Iglesia de Jesús has a gilded Baroque interior, with intricate frescoes and vaulted ceilings, which contrast strikingly with the simplicity of the nearby Franciscan churches. On the exterior, look out for traces of carvings on some of the stones – these were taken from Maya temples.

The charming facade of Campeche Cathedral

9 Campeche Cathedral

A5

The central facade of this cathedral was completed in the 1600s, but its towers were added later – the left one in the 1750s, and the right one as late as the 1850s.

10 Mérida Cathedral

C2

Built by Spanish conquistadors, Mérida's main cathedral was considered extravagant by church leaders of the time. At the entrance to the church, there are statues of saints Peter and Paul.

CITIES AND TOWNS

1 Tizimín

The town's *(p110)* name comes from the Mayan word *tsimin*, a kind of demon, also used to describe the Spaniards when they first appeared on horseback. Its pleasant twin central plazas are divided by two huge monasteries, giving it a distinctly Mediterranean appearance. Today, the town is the capital of Yucatán's "cattle country," located between Valladolid and Río Lagartos.

2 Valladolid

Valladolid *(p108)* combines the elegance of colonial architecture with the easygoing atmosphere of a Yucatán market town. Whitewashed arcades and 17th-century houses surround the main plaza, and among the city's many old Spanish houses and churches is a fine Franciscan monastery *(p52)*. Just off the plaza, Casa de los Venados houses one of Mexico's finest collections of modern folk art. Valladolid is also famous for its unique water source, the dramatic Cenote Zací, just outside the city center.

Twin towers of the historic cathedral at Valladolid

3 Teabo

C4

With an air of pleasant tranquility, this remote town clusters around its grand and lofty Franciscan church, built in 1650–95. In the sacristy are rare murals of saints, discovered by accident in the 1980s. Teabo is also known for its fine embroidery.

4 Ticul

With a friendly atmosphere, Ticul *(p118)* is the epitome of a small Yucatán country town and makes an excellent base for visiting Puuc cities. As well as numerous shops for ceramics, the town's traditional specialty, there is a museum dedicated to chocolate, featuring live demonstrations of Maya ceremonies.

5 Oxkutzcab

C4

In the south of Yucatán near the Puuc Hills is Oxkutzcab, a fertile, fruit-producing region. The town has a huge market *(p79)*, where Maya women in *huípiles* (white blouses with bright embroidery) preside over stalls stacked with succulent mangoes, papaya, oranges, watermelons, and more. Above them stands the lofty tower of the town church, finished in 1645.

6 Acanceh

This remarkable town *(p118)*, featuring a pyramid and a stucco palace, was one of the key northern strongholds of the Yucatán Peninsula during the height of Maya civilization. Today, it showcases over 2,000 years of history, including ancient Maya structures and a fine 18th-century Spanish church.

7 Mérida

The charming capital *(p40)* of the Yucatán, Mérida was founded by the Spaniards in 1542 on the site of the ancient Maya city of Ti'ho. Whitewashed Spanish houses with shaded patios

Brightly colored buildings lining a street in Izamal

provide delightful places to stay. Despite the bustle of its market (and traffic), amid the city's old squares daily life still proceeds at a leisurely, friendly pace.

8 Campeche

The most complete Spanish walled city in Mexico, Campeche *(p46)* is full of reminders of the era when it was a trading hub of Spain's empire. The old city – complete with its churches, patios, Andalusian-style windows, and facades in pastel colors – has been restored to refresh its distinctive Hispanic character.

9 Izamal

Known as *La Ciudad Dorada* (the Golden City) because of the ocher hue of its buildings, this is the most complete and well-preserved colonial town *(p108)* in the Yucatán. At its heart is the largest of the Yucatán's Franciscan monasteries *(p52)*, and a short distance from here are the pyramids of a much older Maya city.

10 Maní

C4

Now wonderfully tranquil, Maní was an important center at the time of the Spanish invasion. It is home to the oldest Franciscan missionary monastery *(p52)* in the Yucatán, and was the site of dramatic events in 1542 when local lords accepted Spanish authority. The monastery and town square are situated on the top of an old Maya temple-platform.

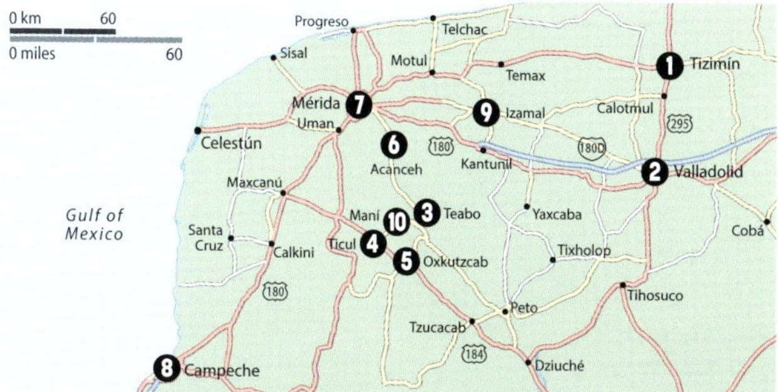

BEACHES

1 Cancún
This resort *(p22)* has the longest stretch of beach, backed by the biggest hotels and malls, and with the most attractions, ranging from parasailing to water parks. The beaches on the north side of the island are the best for swimming and beach life, but they can get rather crowded. On the surf beaches along the east it is always possible to find a spot to yourself, but check safety conditions.

2 Puerto Morelos
Despite its location between Cancún and Playa del Carmen, Puerto Morelos *(p85)* has avoided big-scale development. There's plenty of space along the long, white beach, where pelicans hang in the wind. A great snorkeling reef *(p67)* lies close to the shore.

3 Cozumel
The island of Cozumel *(p24)* is a popular destination among divers, cruise passengers, and families looking for the perfect beach vacation. The finest diving locations are located on the distant reefs, but the tranquil beaches along Cozumel's west coast are ideal for beginners to enjoy a first-time snorkeling and scuba diving experiences. Visitors also flock to the historic town of San Miguel, drawn by its charming and laid-back vibe.

4 Playa del Carmen
This popular spot *(p26)* on the Riviera Maya offers a variety of activities, including shopping, strolling, bar-hopping, and people-watching. It also has miles of lovely palm-lined bays with impressive views stretching to the north. To the south, the Playacar development has its own narrower beaches.

...ng through ...s off Puerto Morelos

Palm trees lining the white-sand beach at Akumal

5 Akumal

This is a lovely area *(p96)* that extends through beautiful, sweeping bays of white sands and gentle seas. Some big hotels have opened, but secluded and low-key condominium apartments and villas can be found located along most of the bays. It's also an excellent diving center *(p67)*.

6 Isla Mujeres

Isla's small size *(p30)* means it has a more laid-back beach scene, especially on Playa Norte by Isla Town, with its placid, safe waters. The island is a good-value diving center.

7 Tulum

This is the favorite spot *(p32)* in the Yucatán for those looking to relax in a palm-roofed cabin by the beach. Head to the north end for affordable cabins where you will get to know your neighbors, or turn south for more secluded and comfortable cabins.

8 Celestún

Most tourists go to Celestún *(p115)* only to see its flamingos, but it is also a tranquil village with a seemingly endless white-sand beach lined by fishing boats. There are some very enjoyable beach restaurants and often wonderful sunsets over the Gulf of Mexico.

9 Isla Holbox

One of the most popular destinations in the Yucatán, particularly among backpackers, Isla Holbox *(p85)* has attractive beaches along the Gulf of Mexico. From May to mid-September, the waters surrounding the island are home to endangered whale sharks, which can be spotted on boat and snorkeling trips. This car-free island is also a favorite among bird-watchers; its shallow lagoon is an ideal place to spot flamingos, pelicans, and other migratory birds.

10 Puerto Aventuras

This Mediterranean-style resort town *(p95)*, built in the late 1990s around a natural inlet along the coast, is home to the Riviera's best-equipped yachting marina. The marina is surrounded by a stylish holiday village featuring villas and condo apartments. A wide range of recreational activities are offered here, including swimming, scuba diving, snorkeling, and deep-sea fishing. The town also has a golf course, tennis center, and several excellent hotels offering top-notch amenities.

A flock of flamingos near Celestún

Exploring the upper chambers of the Dos Ojos Cenote

ECO-PARKS AND THEME PARKS

1 Aqua World, Cancún

K5 Blvd Kukulcán, km 15.2 7am–8pm daily aquaworld.com.mx

A multi-activity fun center on Cancún Island, Aqua World offers a wide range of experiences, including jungle tours, submarine rides, snorkeling, diving, fishing, parasailing, dinner cruises, dolphin watching, and tours to Isla Mujeres and Cozumel. The SubSee Explorer is a great option for non-swimmers and children. Note, charges apply for each activity.

2 Canamayte Cenote and Ecopark, Tulum

P6 Terreno Parcelario, Rancho Viejo (998) 870 5167 9am–5pm daily

One of the region's lesser-visited eco-parks, this hidden gem is one of the most beautiful spots in Tulum. It offers magnificent views of lush land-scapes and plenty of wildlife. The park is home to two great cenotes: Chen Ha and Mariposa. These stunning cenotes have pools of clear water, perfect for a refreshing dip. Afterward, you can refuel at the on-site bar and restaurant.

3 Dos Ojos Cenote, Tulum

"Dos Ojos," meaning "two eyes," is named for its two interconnected cenotes *(p99)*. Part of the world's longest underwater cave system, the site's upper chambers are a highlight of the Yucatán's most exciting diving tours. Visitors can snorkel or scuba dive through crystal-clear cave waters in giant arched-roof caverns.

4 Parque Garrafón, Isla Mujeres

L2 Carretera Garrafón, km 6 10am–5pm Tue–Sun garrafon.com

The main attraction at this park is a broad, natural pool made of rock and coral. There's also a swimming pool, and snorkeling reefs just offshore. The calm waters make it good for novices, while hiking and biking trails offer a change of scene. Visitors can also enjoy a wide range of recreational activities here, including kayaking, paddleboarding, snorkeling, and zip-lining. Those looking for a more relaxed experience can unwind in the infinity pool or decompress in the *temazcal* (Maya sweat lodge).

5 Xplor, Playa del Carmen

Located 4 miles (6 km) south of Playa del Carmen, Xplor *(p86)* is the Riviera Maya's biggest adventure park. Fourteen ziplines, including Cancún's longest, take visitors soaring above the jungle canopy to splashdown landings in cool, cenote waters. Visitors can drive amphibious vehicles across rope bridges and through grottoes and jungle, paddle a raft on warm, clear waters through subterranean caverns, and swim along underground rivers amid stalactites and stalagmites.

6 Aktun-Chen, Akumal

From the highway near Akumal, a dirt track leads west through thick bromeliad-filled jungle to a nature park set around a vast cave *(p99)* and cenote system. Swim and zipline across the cenote and take guided tours through the stalactite-filled cavern, which is highly impressive. Colorful birds, monkeys, and wild boars can be seen outside.

7 Chankanaab, Cozumel

R5 Carretera Costera Sur, km 9 (987) 872 1522 8am–4pm Mon–Fri

This small nature and snorkeling park lies close to the Chankanaab and Paraíso reefs *(p67)* and includes a beach, a botanical garden, and a spa. Activities such as scuba diving and snorkeling are also available.

Enjoying a dip at Chankanaab in Cozumel

8 Xel-Ha, Tulum

One of the Riviera's most popular attractions, this snorkel park *(p96)* was created around a magnificent natural coastal lagoon. The park is especially good for children and has a special area called the Children's World where the little ones can have their own adventures. It may seem crowded at first, but if you swim a bit away from the landing stages, you'll still find plenty of fish and coral to admire in peace. There are also some lovely forest trails to explore.

9 Xplor Fuego, Playa del Carmen

Q4 Carretera Chetumal, Puerto Juarez, km 282 5:30–11pm Mon–Sat xcaret.com

This Playa del Carmen-based park operates at night only. It offers jungle rides on amphibious vehicles, ziplining under the stars, and swimming or boating through stalactite-studded caves. An all-you-can-eat buffet is available from 6:30pm onward. Be sure to book tickets online in advance.

10 Xcaret, Playa del Carmen

The Riviera's original eco-park *(p87)* provides a spectacular introduction to the richness and variety of a tropical environment.

WILDLIFE RESERVES

1 Isla Contoy

This uninhabited island reserve *(p86)* north of Isla Mujeres is home to a huge range of seabirds, including pelicans, boobies, and frigate birds, and contains mangroves, turtle-breeding beaches, and superb coral lagoons. One-day tours are run by many dive shops and agencies from Isla and Cancún; check what is included in your tour.

2 Campeche Petenes

The north of Campeche State behind the coast consists of *petenes, (p118)* which are "islands" of solid land within the swamp that have special microclimates all of their own, and mangrove lagoons. The expansive area is home to various animals, including flamingos, deer, and even pumas. While visitor facilities are very limited, boats to the "islands" can be hired from the village of Isla Arena.

3 Puerto Morelos

The reef off Puerto Morelos *(p85)* is one of the least disturbed sections of coral near the mainland in the northern part of the Maya reef and is now protected as a marine park. Snorkelers can see spectacular marine life – lobsters, giant sponges, luminous parrot fish, and angelfish. Dive operators in the town offer low-impact snorkel and diving tours.

4 Punta Laguna

Spider monkeys are quite common in the Yucatán but often hard to see. Set in very dense forest around a lake near Cobá, this village-run reserve *(p99)* is one of the places to find them. Monkeys are most commonly spotted in the early morning and early afternoon. For the best chance to see them in their natural habitat, take a guided tour of the reserve.

5 Sian Ka'an Biosphere Reserve

Biggest by far of the Yucatán's nature reserves, this vast expanse *(p34)* of empty forest, mangroves, and lagoons gives an extraordinary glimpse of nature almost untouched by human habitation, and in all its complexity. Tulum is the starting point for organized trips into the reserve.

Boat-billed heron, at the Sian Ka'an Biosphere Reserve

Lake and turquoise sea on either side at Punta Sur Eco Beach Park

6 Río Lagartos

A huge, long, narrow lagoon of creeks, mangroves, and mud and salt flats runs along the north coast of Yucatán and it is tinged pink with colonies of 20,000 flamingos in the peak August breeding season. Fascinating, great-value boat trips are run from Río Lagartos *(p108)* and nearby San Felipe *(p107)*.

7 Bocas de Dzilam

D1

Much more remote, this giant expanse of uninhabited mangrove lagoons extends west of San Felipe and also contains flamingo colonies and a variety of birds and other undisturbed wildlife. Getting there is an adventure in itself, with a boat trip across open sea. Boat captains from Rió Lagartos *(p108)*, San Felipe *(p107)*, and Dzilam Bravo can be hired to take you through the mangrove lagoons, with trips lasting a full day.

8 Punta Sur Eco Beach Park, Cozumel

R6 Carretera Costera Sur, km 27
9am–5pm Mon–Sat

This large area across the southern tip of Cozumel has an impressive variety of landscapes – forest, dunes, turtle beaches, reefs, and tranquil mangrove lagoons – plus crocodiles, flamingos, and countless other birds. The area features observation towers, an information center, and a maritime museum. Visitors can climb the Punta Celaraín lighthouse to enjoy stunning panoramic views of the landscape.

9 Celestún Biosphere Reserve

A3

The most famous flamingo colonies in the Yucatán are in the lagoon beside the little town of Celestún *(p115)* on the west coast. Launches run from a visitor center toward the pink streaks of flamingos on the horizon, passing fishers' huts and ibises and many other birds along the way – an ornithologist's delight.

10 Uaymitún

C2

For easy bird-watching in the lagoons along the northern Yucatán coast, this free viewing tower by the coast road east of Progreso is a good option; it even provides binoculars to get a closer look at the local wildlife. The top of the tower offers spectacular views over the wetlands to the south, and you can see flamingos, ducks, egrets, and, in winter, countless migratory birds from North America.

CENOTES AND CAVES

1 Cenote and Eco-Park Kantun-Chi

There are several cenotes on the landward side of the highway near Xpu-Ha that can be easily accessed by visitors. One of the best for a refreshing swim is the Kantun-Chi cenote *(p88)*, a broad, shady pool dappled by brilliant sunlight, located near to the road. The neighboring cenotes of Cristalino and Azul are also beautiful.

2 Cenote Samula

Beyond the narrow entrance to this cenote, there's a huge pool of cool, clear water *(p107)*. Inside the cave, the roots of a giant ceiba tree – revered by the Maya for its mystical powers – stretch straight down from the surface to reach the water far below. Visitors can place their belongings in lockers and take a dip in the water.

3 Dos Ojos Cenote

This cavern *(p99)* is called "Two Eyes" because its two entrances look like eyes when seen from above. Extending over 350 miles (563 km) through a labyrinth of caverns and limestone "trees," it has been considered the world's longest underwater cave system – but the nearby Nohoch Nah Chich cenote may be even longer. Inexperienced divers get the most out of it by joining diving tours.

4 Balankanché Caves

Alongside several cenote pools and underwater rivers, the Yucatán is underlain by a massive web of dry caves that were sacred places to the ancient Maya. Balankanché *(p107)*, near Chichén Itzá, is one of the largest and most extraordinary cave systems of all.

5 Sacred Cenote, Chichén Itzá

The most celebrated cenote in the Yucatán, the giant sacred well at Chichén Itzá *(p36)* has long been said to have been a place of human sacrifice. The cenote was used only for ritual purposes, perhaps as a channel to the Underworld, since

the city's drinking water came from the Xtoloc Cenote, near the Caracol.

6 Cenote Xlacah, Dzibilchaltún

The wide cenote that provided water for the ancient city of Dzibilchaltún *(p116)* is still a popular swimming hole today. It gets busy on Sundays but is great for a dip at other times.

7 Calcehtok

B3

These caves near the Maya site at Oxkintok *(p118)* are little known but are some of the region's most extraordinary. The roofless main chamber is big enough to contain whole trees, and is full of birds.

8 Gran Cenote

The loveliest of the several cenotes along the road from Tulum to Cobá, Gran Cenote *(p98)* is home to a placid, clear pool. Snorkelers and divers can make their way through a massive arched cavern and down a tunnel.

9 Cenote Dzitnup

The most famous of the swimmable cenotes in the region, this awe-inspiring limestone cavern *(p107)* has a perfect turquoise pool. Access is through a narrow tunnel, leading to steep steps that descend into the underground pool. Here, a hole in the roof, along with electric lighting, illuminate the setting. Visitors can also swim among the fish in the clear water. Guided tours usually start at about 11am, but at other times the site is rarely crowded.

10 Loltún Caves

An astonishing cave system, Loltún Caves *(p117)* is not far from the Puuc cities *(p45)*. These caves have the longest history of human habitation in the Yucatán. The chambers here are full of bizarre and interesting rock formations, strange airflows, and relics of their Maya occupants.

Swimming in the Sacred Cenote at Chichén Itzá

SPORTS AND OUTDOOR ACTIVITIES

1 Golf

Golfers on the Riviera have a choice of two championship-level courses at the Club de Golf Cancún *((987) 267 9653)* and Puerto Aventuras Golf Club *(puertoaventuras.com)*. There's also the scenic Greg Norman-designed El Camaleón at Mayakoba, Latin America's first PGA golf course.

2 Diving

The Maya Riviera is home to the world's second-largest reef. Scuba Total *(scubatotal.com)*, a family-run and environmentally conscious dive operator, is committed to making diving accessible to everyone.

3 Sailing, Windsurfing, and Kayaking

The best places to rent boats are Isla Mujeres and Cozumel. Hotels may have dinghies available for use by guests. A day's sailing is a great way to explore lesser-known stretches of the coast. Windsurfing is at its finest around Isla Mujeres and Akumal, and the best spots for kayaking are around Puerto Morelos and Punta Solimán.

4 Fishing

Conditions for deep-sea and inshore fishing in the Yucatán are outstanding, and the lagoons south of the Riviera by Ascencion Bay are a must for fly-fishing fans. The peak deep-sea fishing season runs from March to June.

5 Stand-Up Paddleboarding

Explore the waterways and seas with this increasingly popular activity. While gear can be rented for self-guided excursions, beginners should consider starting first with a guided trip. The calm waters of the region's lagoons are ideal for such trips. 360 SUP-Kayak Tour Cancún *(supcancun.com)* offers guided tours through the Laguna Nichupté *(p22)* – no prior experience is required.

6 Tennis

Tennis courts abound in and around Cancún, but the 2018 opening of the Rafa Nadal Tennis Center *(rafanadaltenniscentre.com)*, with its eight clay courts, raised the bar. Most hotels also have on-site courts, with some, like the RIU Caribe Hotel *(riu.com)*, open to the public.

Swimming and kayaking at Playa Norte in Isla Mujeres

Cycling along the scenic coastline in Tulum

7 Cycling

The most attractive towns for cycling are Cancún, Isla Mujeres, Tulum, and Valladolid, which has a lovely cycle path to Cenote Dzitnup *(p107)*. Many Cancún hotels have bikes, and there are rental shops in the other three destinations.

8 Skydiving

There are a number of places to skydive in the Yucatán. Sky Dive Playa *(skydive.com.mx)* offers visitors a bird's-eye view of the Riviera as they plummet down harnessed to an instructor, or on their own if they already have suitable skydiving experience.

9 Soccer

Mexicans love soccer and locals can be seen playing in towns and beaches across the Yucatán. If you're more a spectator than a player, grab tickets to catch Cancún FC *(cancunfc.com)* in action – the local soccer team, founded in 2020, plays at the Olímpico Andrés Quintana Roo Stadium.

10 Yoga

Yoga is becoming increasingly popular, with classes held in towns and wellness resorts throughout the region. Head to the nearest studio for some sessions of mindfulness or try the unique stand-up paddle-boarding class offered by Yin Yoga SUP *(yinyogasup.com)*.

TOP 10 DIVING REEFS

1. Manchones, Isla Mujeres
L2
A fascinatingly varied reef, half a mile (1 km) long, but only around 30 ft (9 m) deep for much of its length.

2. Tankah
This less well-known beach *(p98)* is great for relaxed snorkeling and diving away from the crowds.

3. Paraíso, Cozumel
R5
Cozumel offers the greatest extent and variety of reef for snorkelers and divers of every level, with excellent visibility throughout.

4. Puerto Morelos
The reef in this town *(p85)* is located unusually close to the shore, making it ideal for snorkel tours and introductory diving.

5. Akumal
Akumal *(p96)* is an important cave-diving center, with its reefs offering excellent opportunities for snorkeling and diving.

6. Tulum
This resort town *(p32)* is the Riviera's biggest center for cave-diving, offering snorkelers and divers the chance to explore reefs in its waters.

7. Reefs around Cancún
Despite the relatively small size of the closest reefs, there's still lots to see. "Jungle" snorkeling tours pass through mangroves in Laguna Nichupté *(p22)* and to the reef off Punta Nizuc.

8. Playa del Carmen and Chunzubul
Several high-standard dive operators are based in Playa *(p26)*, taking divers to the reefs nearby.

9. Palancar, Cozumel
Q6
An extraordinary coral mountain with giant canyons that plunge from the surface to the depths of the ocean.

10. Xpu-Ha
Angelfish, triggerfish, and parrot fish are abundant in the reefs here *(p97)*, along with a luxuriant range of coral.

Enjoying the view from the pier at Punta Allen

OFF THE BEATEN PATH

1 Punta Allen

G5

The poor condition of the road to Punta Allen keeps visitor numbers low, but the trek deep into Sian Ka'an *(p34)* (accessible only by four-wheel drive) leads to a small fishing village with sand streets and giant palms. The village features stages by the beach, a few restaurants, and welcoming places to stay. Local guides offer snorkeling, bird-watching, and fishing trips.

2 Río Lagartos and San Felipe

Celebrated for the spectacular flocks of flamingos in the lagoon *(p108)* to their east, these villages delight visitors with their unhurried, easygoing style. There are great seafood restaurants too, as well as some pleasant small hotels, and, from San Felipe *(p107)*, wonderful sunsets.

3 Puerto Morelos

An undisturbed gem of the Mexican Caribbean, Puerto Morelos *(p85)* has managed to retain its laid-back, fishing-village charm despite its close proximity to Cancún. While there's no bustling nightlife, the town offers lovely beaches and several offshore diving sites. Turtles can often be spotted along the coastal shores. Visitors will also find a range of small apartments and hotels here that offer long-term rates.

4 Punta Bete

A well-rutted track off the main highway, just north of Playa del Carmen, leads in 2 bumpy miles (3 km) to superb, curving beaches with dazzling white sand and a perfect turquoise sea. Visitors can enjoy activities such as camping, snorkeling, and surfing. While a few resorts and hotels have opened here *(p85)*, there are still peaceful clusters of beachside cabañas tucked away among the palms, offering a quiet escape.

5 Isla Holbox

If the Riviera seems too busy, take a long drive north to the tiny port of Chiquilá. Hop on a ferry to cross the beautiful lagoon, where dolphins are often spotted gliding through the crystal-clear waters, to reach the island of Holbox *(p85)*. Here you'll find the simple pleasures of a friendly village, a long, empty beach, and some mellow places to stay. The island is also a hot spot for various adventure activities such as snorkeling, diving, and kiteboarding.

6 Akumal

Though not exactly remote, the curving beaches of Akumal *(p96)* are very long and often occupied only by a few small-scale hotels and condo apartments. It's quite easy to find uncrowded spots along the coastline, with modern amenities available. There's abundant sea life to explore, with stingrays, barracudas, and vibrant tropical fish gliding through the waters. There are also excellent diving facilities here.

7 El Cuyo

With just one hotel, two sets of beach cabañas, and a couple of places to eat (serving delicious fresh fish), this Gulf coast fishing village *(p110)* is for anyone who really does want a beach all to themselves. Beyond relaxing on the beach, visitors can also try their hand at kitesurfing or wander through the village to explore its buildings.

8 Bacalar

Several hours south of Tulum, just north of Mexico's border with Belize, is Bacalar, one of Mexico's Pueblos Mágicos, or Magical Towns. Often referred to as the "Maldives of Mexico," this spot is known for its "Seven Colors Lagoon," an enchanting place where seven colors of blue-green can be seen in the water. The town is also home to a piracy museum, which showcases a collection of artifacts and weapons.

The serene Seven Colors Lagoon at Bacalar

9 Celestún

Flamingos are the big attraction here *(p115)* but, if you stay overnight in one of the small hotels after the day-trippers have returned to Mérida, you will be able to make the most of the quiet charm of this peaceful village. Its beach, dotted with fishing boats, is a great spot for relaxing. Along the shore, there's a 19th-century lighthouse that's well worth a visit. North of Celestún is a somewhat remote beach retreat at Xixim.

10 Hacienda Hotels

An enticing escape is offered (at upscale prices) by the hotels scattered around the Yucatán in beautifully converted old colonial country estates. These hotels incorporate architectural features such as intricate tilework, arched doorways, and lovely open courtyards with fountains, all reminiscent of the style of traditional haciendas *(p133)*. All have luxurious rooms surrounded by tropical gardens, with superb pools and fine restaurants.

FAMILY ATTRACTIONS

1 Parque Ecoturístico Kaalmankal, Tekax

C4 Calle 70, Carretera Tekax-Kancab, km 1 (999) 251 8895

The remote town of Tekax is home to an eco-park set amid the scenic hills that surround the area. Visitors can camp under a stunning night sky that's filled with stars on clear nights. During the day, the park offers numerous activities, including guided tours of caves, family-friendly rappelling, ziplining, and a ride on the Kaalmankal swing.

2 Xcaret, Playa del Carmen

The first and most famous of the eco-parks, Xcaret *(p87)* provides lots for kids to enjoy, in an easy, family-centered environment *(p28)*. The snorkeling river is a big hit, but children can also enjoy the Coral Reef Aquarium, explore the butterfly garden, and wander along forest paths. A part of the park has been created especially for children and has, among other things, water slides, hanging bridges, and tunnels.

3 Río Secreto, Playa del Carmen

This amazing underground cave and river system *(p88)* is located just south of Playa del Carmen. Don a wet suit and helmet to explore the river that flows 82 ft (25 m) below the surface and see the many spectacular stalagmites and stalactites.

4 Xel-Ha, Playa del Carmen

This snorkel park *(p96)* is one of the Riviera's top family attractions. The coral lagoon is a favorite among kids, offering the perfect setting for swimming, snorkeling, and exploring the surrounding lush forest.

5 Xcacel Beach

Seven of the world's eight marine turtle species nest on the shores of the Yucatán, including green sea and loggerhead turtles. The turtles, many of which are endangered, are vigorously protected by Mexican authorities, and many of the Yucatán's nesting areas have been turned into reserves and sanctuaries. At several of these spots, visitors can help biologists and other officials during nesting season, including at Xcacel Beach *(p88)*, just 40 minutes south of Playa del Carmen.

6 Punta Laguna

Getting to see local wildlife in its natural habitat, rather than in zoos or nature parks, can take time and effort, but at this small reserve *(p99)* north of Cobá village guides lead the way and you can see spider monkeys jumping through the trees after just a little exciting exploration. Deer, wild boar, and lots of birds can likely be seen, too.

7 Chankanaab, Cozumel

This is one of the most enjoyable and accessible places *(p61)* for even small children to be dazzled by a first introduction to snorkeling and the underwater treasures of the Cozumel reefs. The sea is very placid, and there's coral and abundant sea life just off the beach. There's also a coral lagoon in the same park.

8 Uxmal

Especially popular with kids, Uxmal *(p42)* is an ancient Maya site. Not only does it have plenty of steps and temples for running around, but it is also home to many iguanas, which sit stock still until surprised, then dart off with sudden alacrity. Some are as big as crocodiles, but they're all harmless. Unlike most Yucatán sites, Uxmal has no cenotes, and instead, water was stored in *chultunes* (artificial cisterns). The most striking monument here is the Pyramid of the Magician, with its tall, steep structure set on an unusual oval base. According to legend, it was built in a single night by a dwarf with supernatural powers – known as the Magician.

Relaxing in the tranquil lagoon at Xel-Ha

Admiring the Pyramid of the Magician at Uxmal

9 Laguna Yal-Ku, Akumal

P5 8am–6pm daily

This winding rock pool of brilliant turquoise water, right at the north end of Akumal's Media Luna Bay *(p103)*, is one of the natural coral inlets on the Riviera coast. Rarely crowded, it's delightful for swimming and snorkeling with young children, with coral and colorful fish that are easy to spot.

10 Playa Mia, Cozumel

R6 Dawn–dusk daily

Cozumel's beach clubs offer all the fun of the sand and sea, plus restaurants and loungers in the shade. Playa Mia has the best choice of things to do for older children – snorkeling, beach games, kayaks, and banana boats – and it has a kid's club for little ones.

NIGHTS OUT

1 Live Music in Mérida

Every night of the week, the streets of Mérida *(p40)* are filled with music, led by the famous *trovadores (p41)*. They can be seen in Plaza Grande and Plaza Mayor on most evenings, and at the Thursday *trova* event in Parque Santa Lucía. Alternatively, pop into one of Mérida's cantinas, such as El Cardenal *(Calle 63 527, Parque Santiago)*, where you'll often find live music and salsa dancing.

2 Clubs

Cancún is justifiably famous for its club scene. Choose between mega spots like the 6,000-capacity Mandala or the iconic Coco Bongo *(p91)*, with its DJ sets, acrobats, and samba-inspired performances. It's not the only place to party, though. Nearby Playa del Carmen is also a hot spot, with buzzy clubs like La Vaquita *(p91)*, where reggaeton and hip-hop rule.

3 Theater

The Yucatán has long been a hub of cultural arts, with many playwrights hailing from here. The state's most famous theater, Teatro Peón Contreras (reopening in late 2025) in Mérida, has a variety of shows and is home to the Yucatán Symphony Orchestra *(sinfonicadeyucatan.com.mx)*. Elsewhere, the Riviera Maya has a number of theaters including one in the Vidanta Resort *(p130)*, which hosts the Cirque du Soleil.

4 Traditional Celebrations

Spiritual, soul-seeking types can observe Maya customs here, including the ritual to the goddess of love and fertility, Ixchel, at Zazil Tunich *(zaziltunich.com)* and a cacao ceremony in Tulum with Medicine Wheel *(medicinewheel.mx)*. You can also experience a cleansing rebirth in a "sweat lodge" as part of the *temazcal* ceremony at Dune Escapism, Tulum *(dunehoteltulum.com)*.

5 Beach Clubs

With plenty of great beach spots in the Yucatán, you don't need to leave the coast to party here. Enjoy big nights at Cancún's Mandala Beach Club *(mandalatickets.com)* and the Chicabal Sunset Club *(p91)*. More relaxed nights can be had with a sundowner in hand at Ziggy's Beach Club *(ziggybeachtulum.com)* in Tulum.

6 Family Activities

While the region attracts revelers, there's still plenty to keep little ones entertained after sundown. Seek outdoor adventures in the jungle of Xplor Fuego park *(p61)* or stay indoors at Salón

Crowds standing in line to enter Coco Bongo nightclub

Gallos *(salongallos.mx)*, with its gallery, movie theater, and restaurant. If you're lucky, a visit to Mérida will coincide with La Noche Blanca, a biannual arts festival (usually in May and November) with a packed agenda of free concerts, performances, and exhibitions.

7 Nighttime Kayaking

Grab a paddle and join a guided evening tour of the Yucatán's waterways. Spot wildlife at sunset in the Sian Ka'an Biosphere Reserve *(p34)* with the sustainably run Yucatán Outdoors *(yucatanoutdoors.com/tour)*, or explore the mangrove channels of Chuburná Puerto with one of the local operators *(chuburnayucatan.com/tour-operators)*.

8 Bars

This is a region that doesn't lack for great bars. Cancún and Cozumel are ideal for first-timers with places like Señor Frog's *(p92)* and Carlos'n Charlie's *(p104)* providing the party vibes. For a more authentic Mexican evening, visit the cantinas in Mérida – Arcano *(arcano.rest)* and La Negrita Cantina *(p120)* are among the best.

9 Light-and-Sound Shows

When the sun sets, the Yucatán is lit up with fantastic light projections. The shows, which last from 15 to 90 minutes, beam amazing displays onto buildings and structures, including the convent in Izamal *(p108)*, the Monumento a la Patria in Mérida *(p40)*, and the pyramid of Kukulcán at Chichén Itzá *(p36)*. Best of all, most shows are free.

10 Sunset Sailing in Cancún

The warm climate and mesmeric sunsets make cruising a great option. You can charter a boat, but it's more fun to join a tour ship with a history theme: the Columbus Romantic cruise *(columbuscancun.com.mx)* is aboard a galleon, and Captain Hook's Pirate Night *(p91)* is, of course, on a pirate ship.

TOP 10 **DRINKS**

1. Beer
Mexico produces several well-known beers, including Corona, Dos Equis, and Negra Modelo.

2. Tequila
Mexico's national drink is made by distilling the fermented juices of the blue agave, and forms the base of many cocktails.

3. Horchata
A traditional drink said to be a cure for hangovers. It's a mix of sugar, almonds, and cinnamon and is usually served with ice.

4. Wine
Mexico produces over 40 varieties of wines, available at most bars and restaurants in the Yucatán.

5. Pulque
This alcoholic drink can be traced back to ancient times. It's made from the fermented sap of the *maguey*.

6. Michelada
Part beer, part cocktail, this unique drink is the result of combining beer, Worcester sauce, tomato juice, chili, soy sauce, lime juice, and salt.

7. Atole
A traditional hot drink made from *masa* (corn starch) with different flavors such as vanilla and guava.

8. Xtabentún
A uniquely Yucatecán drink that uses honey made by bees that feed on the *xtabentún* plant and combines it with anise seed.

9. Licuados
Mix fruit juice with milk, honey, and yogurt, and the result is this cross between a milkshake and a smoothie.

10. Aguas Frescas
The popular soft drink blends fruit with chilled water. It's the perfect refreshing drink during the summer months.

A traditional version of aguas frescas

LOCAL DISHES

1 Cochinita Pibil

This dish dates back to pre-Conquest Maya cooking – pork marinated in lime, bitter orange, and *achiote* (a mild spice with a slightly peppery taste), wrapped in banana leaves and baked in a *pib*, an earthen pit. While some restaurants now prepare the dish in an earthenware pot, the traditional pit-cooking method remains popular.

2 Puchero

Commonly eaten as a Sunday lunch, *puchero* is a hearty stew found across Latin America, but with its origins in Spain. In the Yucatán Peninsula it is typically packed with pork, beef, chicken, and vegetables, spiced with allspice and cinnamon, and finished off with a garnish of diced habañero peppers, oranges, cilantro, and radishes.

3 Poc-Chuc

Marinating is one of the most characteristic skills of Yucatecan cooking, and this delicious dish features pork marinated in the juice of *naranja agria* (small, bitter oranges, special to the region), cooked with onions, herbs, and garlic, and served with black beans. With a wonderful mix of sweet and savory flavors, it's very popular, but debate rages as to whether it is really traditional or a creation of La Chaya Maya restaurant *(p121)* in Mérida.

***Poc-chuc*, a popular traditional Yucatán pork dish**

4 Pollo Oriental de Valladolid

The pride of Valladolid: chicken quartered on the bone and casseroled with garlic, onion, cloves, and a mix of both hot and mild chilis; it's then quickly roasted in a baste of maize oil and bitter orange juice. This is another regional dish with a rich, densely layered combination of different flavors. *Pavo oriental* is the turkey version.

5 Relleno Negro

In *relleno negro* ("black stuffing"), finely ground pork, peppers, grated hard-boiled egg, herbs, spices, and a powerful combination of chilis are mixed together to make up a thick, majestic sauce. It is usually served with *pavo* or *guajolote* (turkey), the region's traditional meat.

6 Pollo con Mole

This dish is a central Mexican classic. The chicken is covered in *mole*, a thick, spicy, savory chocolate sauce. Richly satisfying, this is one of the oldest uses of chocolate, its flavor uniting perfectly with strongly spiced meats.

7 Camarón al Mojo de Ajo

All around the coast, fish and seafood are restaurant staples. One of the simplest and most delicious ways of cooking the likes of *camarón* (prawns/shrimp) and *caracol* (conch) is *al mojo de ajo*, fried quickly in hot oil with lots of garlic.

Bowl of delicious *sopa de lima* soup

8 Sopa de Lima

One of the most popular classics of Yucatecan cooking, this "lime soup" is actually made with chicken, boned and chopped into strips, and then slow-cooked with cilantro, onions, herbs, spices, and masses of local sweet limes. It's served with thinly sliced strips of crispy, fried tortillas, adding the perfect crunch.

9 Crepas de Chaya

Tasting like spinach, *chaya* is a vegetable native to the Yucatán. It features in traditional cooking and contemporary dishes such as this one. It is cooked with garlic and wrapped in light, European-style wheat pancakes (crêpes) and served with a cheese sauce. *Chaya* is also used to make drinks.

10 Arroz con Pulpo

Arroz con pulpo is a Campeche specialty: a delicious, warm salad that's much lighter than most other local dishes and perfect for a hot day. Rice *(arroz)* is mixed together with finely chopped octopus *(pulpo)*, red peppers, onion, cilantro, and other herbs. Mango, papaya, or other seasonal fruits are often added to the dish to give it a refreshing blend of sweet juice and salty seafood flavors.

TOP 10 YUCATECAN SNACKS AND STREET FOODS

1. Ceviche
Raw fish or seafood marinated in lemon or lime juice, and served with salad, spices, and lots of cilantro.

2. Cócteles
Fish or seafood ceviches, served in a glass, typically paired with a tangy, flavorful vinaigrette-style dressing.

3. Papadzules
A Maya dish of chopped hard-boiled eggs in a sweet pumpkin-seed sauce, rolled in tortillas and often served with a spicy tomato sauce.

4. Panuchos
Small, crisp-fried tortillas covered in refried beans and topped with strips of chicken or turkey, plus generous helpings of chopped tomato, onion, avocado, and chilis.

5. Salbutes
Similar to *panuchos*, but made with a thicker, spongier base instead of crisp tortillas.

6. Enchiladas
In southern Mexico, these rolled soft tortillas with various fillings tend to be served with a rich *mole* sauce.

7. Tacos
Small rolled tortillas filled with 1,001 possible fillings: at taco stands, they're served rolled up; at *taquerías* you sit and assemble them yourself.

8. Fajitas
Pan-fried meat or seafood served sizzling alongside bowls of onions, refried beans, chili sauce, guacamole, and soft tortillas.

9. Tortas
These delicious sandwiches use a small bread roll and pack it with a variety of different fillings.

10. Quesadillas
Small, soft tortillas that are folded over and filled with melted cheese and occasionally ham. They're usually served up with a range of sweet and savory sauces.

TRADITIONAL CRAFTS AND SOUVENIRS

1 Sisal Mats

The Yucatán was once Mexico's most prosperous state, thanks to the sisal industry, a fiber extracted from the agave plant. One of the many products made with sisal is floor mats, which adorn hotels and haciendas throughout the Yucatán. The woven mats can be purchased in many towns and are a perfect stand-in for rugs or carpets, with simple but beautiful designs that are durable – and easy to roll up to take home with you.

2 Hand-woven Hammocks

Have you really visited the Yucatán if you haven't spent some quality time swinging back and forth in a hammock? These can be traced back to the pre-colonial Maya, who used fibers from the *hamack* tree to construct the first hammocks – hence the name. Today's luxurious versions are made from hand-woven cotton, and the best come from the northern town of Tixkokob, where there are around 30 artisan workshops devoted to hammock craft.

3 Jipijapa Hats

Say that five times fast. *Jipijapa* hats are one of the region's signature hats. Each hat is woven by hand using dried toquilla palm fronds and can take weeks or even months to complete. The tradition dates back more than 200 years and is so prized that the hats have been recognized by UNESCO on their Intangible Cultural Heritage list.

A floral-patterned example of a *jipijapa* hat

4 Guayaberas

Guayaberas are the iconic shirt worn throughout Mexico and Latin America. They originated in Cuba but have since become a fashion staple in Mexican culture thanks to their formal yet elegant look. It also helps that the lightweight fabric is ideal for the hot, humid climate in the Yucatán. Guayaberas are found at many shops and markets across the region, but especially fine selections are available around downtown Mérida *(p40)*, where several outlets are dedicated to them.

5 Pottery

Mexico is famous for its ceramics and the Yucatán is no different. Here, the Maya produced an array of colorful pottery – each used for different roles in society. Such products are still made today, many according to traditional techniques, and are especially common in Ticul *(p118)*. On the town's main thoroughfare *(Calle 23)*, you'll find everything from Maya-inspired sculpted masks to vases and other vessels.

6 Baskets

Hand-weaving straw into baskets is a long-standing part of Yucatecan culture and palm frond baskets can be found all over the peninsula. Visit Casa de Artesanías *(p119)* in Mérida to buy some of the best locally made baskets or take a trip to the town of Pisté where master crafters create colorful baskets, perfect for keeping tortillas warm.

7 Honey

It's a little-known fact that the Yucatán is one of the largest producers of honey in Mexico (Campeche is the other). The tropical conditions, abun-

A collection of artisanal wooden masks

dant vegetation, and unusual melipona bees, a stingless species endemic to the area, have made the local liquid amber famous. The resulting product is one-of-a-kind, with its dark color, unique taste, and high health content. Try it for yourself in the town of Maní *(p55)*, where there are several bee farms.

8 Embroidery

Ancient Maya embroidery consisted of women stringing colorful threads together with thorns and feathers. These skills are still practiced today (thankfully with modern needles rather than thorns) by artisans who have mastered a variety of stitches. Products range from religious items – including gowns, banners, and shrouds – to tablecloths and traditional clothing with intricate designs.

9 Wood Carvings

The art of wood carving can trace its origins back to the Maya period, and despite the Spanish colonization, woodworking has been sustained in many communities, passed down from generation to generation. Regional artisans often sell their hand-hewn items along the roadside and in local markets, but for the best crafts, head to the town of Dzityá, just north of Mérida. This town is renowned for its carved wood products, including sculptures, candlesticks, bowls, and decorative items.

10 Sandals

The Yucatán has long been associated with a regional variety of sandal called *huarache*. Traditionally, these were made from hand-woven leather by farmers and Indigenous peoples, but in the 20th century they became linked with "hippie" culture beyond Mexico. Though other materials have been incorporated into modern designs, classic *huaraches* still use leather. Find the best in Ticul *(p118)* or local markets.

Women crafting embroidered goods

CANCÚN AND THE YUCATÁN FOR FREE

1 Nightlife in Mérida

Each night of the week the city center plays host to a range of live music, dance events, theatrical performances, film screenings, and other entertainment. Check out the latest schedule at the city's tourist office *(p40)* or in the free monthly magazine *Yucatán Today*.

2 MACAY, Mérida

C2 Pasaje de la Revolución
Hours vary, check website
macay.org

Home to an outstanding collection of modern art, the Museo de Arte Contemporáneo Ateneo de Yucatán (MACAY) in Mérida *(p40)* features several fascinating works by leading Yucatecan artists and painters such as Fernando Castro Pacheco and Fernando García Ponce.

3 San Bernardino de Siena, Valladolid

An elegant Franciscan church *(p52)* and former convent, San Bernardino de Siena has a magnificent 18th-century altarpiece. Its beautiful walls are decorated with several evocative 17th-century paintings.

4 Xlapak

The smallest and least visited of the Ruta Puuc archaeological sites, the Maya site of Xlapak *(p118)* features a restored palace with doorways decorated with large, eye-catching Chac (the rain god) masks.

5 Mérida Cathedral

Dating back to the late 16th century, Mérida's *(p40)* imposing cathedral *(p53)* is one of the oldest in Latin America.

6 Palacio Centro Cultural, Campeche

A5 Calle 8, between 55–7, Zona Centro (981) 811 0366 10am–7pm Tue–Sun

Charting the tempestuous history of Campeche, this museum offers multimedia displays and innovative exhibits, including a replica Spanish galleon. Most of the descriptions are in Spanish, with a few also in English. There's also a spectacular sound-and-light show on weekends.

7 Izamal's Crafts Workshops

The small town of Izamal *(p108)* is famous for its spectacular crafts scene, and its wood-carvers, jewelers, hammock-makers, and other artisans are happy to show tourists round their workshops *(p111)*. A map showing the locations of many such workshops is available for free from most hotels in town.

8 Oxkutzcab Market

C4 From 7am daily

This charming colonial-era town *(p54)*, surrounded by fruit and vegetable farms, hosts in its main square one of the liveliest and most colorful markets in the region.

9 Punta Bete Beach

R4

This is one of the most picturesque stretches of sand *(p85)* on the Riviera Maya, and less crowded than many of its neighbors thanks to a road that isn't easily accessed.

10 Carnival

Although it may not match the scale of its more famous Brazilian counterpart, in Mexico's version of Carnival *(p80)* is still a fun, lively and raucous affair. Cancún, Cozumel, and Mérida host the biggest celebrations in the Yucatán region – expect costumed dancers, live music, and plenty of good food and drinks. Events for Carnival usually takes place in the week leading up to Lent.

TOP 10 BUDGET TIPS

Fried tortillas at a food stall

1. Markets and snack stands offer reasonably priced items and are often the most lively places to sample local dishes.

2. Visit in the low-season: May–June and late November–early December offer the best combinations of prices and weather.

3. The extensive public bus system in Cancún is an inexpensive way to travel around.

4. It is more economical to rent a car from a small agency in Mérida than in Cancún.

5. Local free magazines often have discount coupons for hotels, restaurants, and other attractions.

6. Some national monuments offer free admission for Mexican nationals on Sundays. The general admission fee for several museums and historic sites is usually inexpensive for Mexican residents.

7. Many ticket-based attractions (except Maya sites) offer discounts for booking online in advance.

8. Most diving operators offer discounts for larger groups, and advance bookings, or when you book multiple dives at once.

9. Most Riviera Maya bars offer two-for-one deals for at least a few hours each night.

10. Save money by using pesos rather than US dollars.

FESTIVALS AND EVENTS

1 Feast of the Three Kings

Jan 6

The capital of Yucatán's cattle country, Tizimín *(p54)*, hosts one of the region's biggest fiestas – the Fiesta de Reyes – every year. This two-week celebration features a stock fair with traditional music, dancing, colorful parades, and plenty of food and drink.

2 La Candelaria

Feb

Valladolid's *(p108)* main fiesta, the Expo-Feria, centers around the Feast of the Virgin of La Candelaria. The event begins with a lively parade where locals display dazzling embroidered dresses, followed by dancing and concerts. Campeche *(p46)* also hosts a similar celebration, though on a smaller scale.

3 Carnival

Feb/Mar (one week before Lent)

This is the biggest and brightest celebration of the year in the Yucatán. In Cancún and Cozumel the streets fill with music, dancing, food stands, and a little Río-style parading. The biggest Carnival in southern Mexico, though, is in Mérida.

4 Equinoxes

Mar 21 & Sep 21

The visual effects integral to the Maya cities – such as the "descent" of the sun down the serpents on El Castillo at Chichén Itzá *(p37)* and the rising sun striking through the Temple of the Seven Dolls at Dzibilchaltún *(p116)* – were timed to happen on the spring and fall equinoxes. Today, some 80,000 visit Chichén Itzá for the day; the crowds are smaller at Dzibilchaltún.

5 San Miguel Arcángel

Sep 20–29

Cozumel's most important fiesta honors the island's patron saint, St. Michael. Over the nine days that precede his feast day, religious processions are held in town with lively music and dancing.

6 Cristo de las Ampollas

Oct

More solemnly religious than most fiestas, with processions culminating on October 13, when the figure of "Christ of the Blisters" (*Cristo de las Ampollas*), kept in Mérida Cathedral *(p40)*, is carried through town before a mass.

Sugar skull candy on sale for the Day of the Dead

7 Day of the Dead and All Saints' Day

Oct 31–Nov 2

Sugar skulls, dead bread *(pan de muerto)*, *zempazuchitl* flowers, and coffin-shaped decorations are the mark of Mexico's most famous celebration, when people party to honor the dead on Halloween and All Saints' Day *(Todos Santos)*, and families visit cemeteries to picnic by the graves of their departed relatives.

8 Cancún Jazz Festival

Dates vary, check website

W cancunjazz.com

Musicians from Latin America, the US, and Europe – often performing Latin jazz and contemporary fusion – participate in this festival, with many concerts in Parque de las Palapas in Cancún.

9 Mérida en Domingo

All year round

Every week, Mérida hosts a free fiesta, "Mérida on Sunday," when the Plaza Mayor and Calle 60 are closed to traffic to make way for strolling crowds and a range of events. There are displays of *jarana* dancing in front of the City Hall and concerts up and down the street.

10 Village Fiestas

Every village and town in the Yucatán also has its own fiesta, when the streets are decorated with garlands, work ceases, and music is played non-stop. For details, check with tourist offices, look out for posters, or consult local newspapers.

Costumed dancers performing during Carnival

TOP 10 GODS AND SPIRITS OF THE ANCIENT MAYA

1. Itzamná

Itzamná, the god of medicine and supposedly the inventor of writing, was one of the most important deities in the Post-Classic Yucatán.

2. Ixchel

Ixchel is the Maya goddess of fertility, childbirth, and weaving.

3. Maize God

Since maize was central to ancient American culture, the Maize God is one of the foremost gods, created by the First Mother and First Father.

4. Hero Twins

In Maya myths, the twins Hunahpu and Xbalanqué embark on a series of adventures and defy the forces of death on their epic journeys.

5. Earth Lord

The Maya viewed the earth as a living being, which could be either generous or monstrous toward humans. Monstermouth temples *(p44)* are often representations of the Earth Lord.

6. Tlaloc

Tlaloc is a Central Mexican god of rain and war, with strange "goggles" on his eyes.

7. Kukulcán

A powerful bird-serpent, the Central Mexican god Quetzalcóatl was known in the Yucatán as Kukulcán.

8. Vision Serpents

Conduits between men and the gods, the Vision Serpents were summoned up by Maya lords and shamans usually during rituals.

9. Cosmic Turtle

The Cosmic Turtle is a symbol of water and the earth. In the Maya creation myth, the Maize God emerges through a crack in the shell of the cosmic turtle.

10. Chac

Chac, the Maya god of rain and lightning, is easily recognized in carvings by his long, curling snout.

AREA BY AREA

A colorful street in Izamal

CANCÚN AND THE NORTH

Cancún is the great draw at the top of the Riviera Maya, with lavish hotels, shopping and dining of every kind, wild nightclubs, theme parks, and water parks spread out along one of the world's finest beaches. To the south is Playa del Carmen, a trendier, more compact vacation town, and family-friendly eco-parks that provide an introduction to the nature of tropical Yucatán. For a change from resort life, in the same area there are also places where the frenetic pace of modern life still seems far away – in the ever-mellow Puerto Morelos, at the bird reserve on Isla Contoy, and on the lovely Isla Mujeres.

For places to stay in this area, see p130

Palapas on the white sands of Cancún Beach

1 Cancún Beach

L4–K6

Every one of the Riviera's beaches has the same wonderful fine white sand, which stays deliciously cool to the touch, but Cancún's is unquestionably the finest, stretching the whole 14 miles (23 km) of Cancún Island. Along it, in the Hotel Zone, are resort hotels, shopping and entertainment centers, watersports and snorkeling, and fun parks, plus the Maya site of El Rey *(p88)*.

2 Cancún Town

J3

On the mainland at the north end of Cancún Island, Ciudad Cancún, also known as "Downtown," was created at the same time as the Hotel Zone in the 1970s. It has developed an atmosphere of its own, though, and the main drag of Avenida Tulum and the nearby squares and avenues are enjoyable places to explore, with plenty of shopping and great restaurants.

3 Puerto Morelos

R3

This small fishing town was once the largest settlement along this coast before the rise of Cancún. Although a few hotels have sprung up here over the past decade, the town has managed to avoid overdevelopment, retaining its quiet charm, which is much loved by the many expats who own houses here or stay whole winters in its small hotels. There's a beautiful white beach, and a superb reef close offshore, now protected as a marine park. Local dive operators and fishing guides give individual, friendly service.

4 Isla Holbox

G1

The tiny peninsula of Holbox, with its unspoiled beaches and luminous waters, is one of the Yucatán's hippest destinations. Set beside a wide lagoon filled with birds and dolphins, it has a delightfully laid-back village, which can be accessed by a 15-minute ferry ride from Chiquilá (with services running from 6am to 9:30pm). Its sandy streets are lined with many charming hotels and restaurants. There's also a vast beach and, in season, the waters offshore are temporarily home to migrating whale sharks.

5 Punta Bete

R4

Set between the pristine beaches of Puerto Morelos and Playa del Carmen, Punta Bete remains off the beaten path by a bumpy 2-mile (3-km) access road through the jungle. This point is flanked by lines of palm-fringed bays – perfect arcs of dazzling white sand by a turquoise sea. They are shared by a few resort hotels, and far more small-scale, cheaper clusters of beach cabañas.

6 Playa del Carmen

The Riviera's most vibrant street life, by day and night, and its hippest crowds can be found in this resort town *(p26)*. Playa's long-established cool bars and backpackers' haunts mix with modern hotels ranging from big resorts to cozy guesthouses. As well as having wonderful beaches, it's great for diving and snorkeling.

7 Isla Mujeres

Although it's only a short ferry ride away from Cancún, this 5-mile- (8-km-) long island *(p30)*, the first place where Spaniards landed in Mexico in 1517 *(p9)*, has a much more relaxed beach-town vibe, with several restaurants and a good selection of affordable places to stay. Set at its southern tip is the Parque Escultórico Punta Sur, an impressive sculpture park, which is also known for its historic lighthouse. The island is also an excellent diving, snorkeling, and fishing center, with an exciting range of offshore reefs to explore either independently or on a tour.

Enjoying snorkeling at Xcaret

8 Isla Contoy

H1

Mexico's most important seabird reserve, located north of Isla Mujeres, covers the whole of this uninhabited island. Its picturesque terrain is a mix of lush mangroves, beaches, and coral lagoons that are home to over 50 species of birds – they contain turtle breeding grounds too. Day tours are offered by dive shops on Isla Mujeres *(p30)*.

9 Xplor

Q4 Federal Highway 307, km 282 9am–5pm daily (to 8pm Sat & Sun) xplor.travel

A trip to this impressive adventure park is the perfect family outing, offering something exciting for everyone. Seven different routes await, including 14 ziplines; two 3-mile- (5-km-) long amphibious vehicle paths, running along jungle tracks, over rope bridges, and through caves; and two underground river-raft circuits. Visitors can also enjoy swimming through a scenic subterranean river, surrounded by a series of stunning rock formations.

Lighthouse at Punta Sur, Isla Mujeres

10 Xcaret

Q4 Chetumal–Puerto Juarez Highway, km 282 8:30am–10pm daily xcaret.com

The largest of the Riviera's growing number of eco-parks *(p60)*, just south of Playa del Carmen, this sprawling adventure spot *(p28)* provides a great introduction to the tropical environment of the Yucatán. Water bugs of all ages will love the swimming and snorkeling options in the many pools and rivers within the park, while animal aficionados can spend time checking out the fascinating collection of animals and butterflies. Guided tours to Xcaret are available daily from both Cancún and Playa del Carmen.

THE CHICLE BOOM

Long before tourism, this region's biggest business was chewing gum. When gum was first invented in the 19th century it was all made with natural chicle, found in the wild sapodilla trees of the Yucatán. Villages such as Puerto Juárez and Puerto Morelos were all founded as harbors for exporting chicle, brought in by sapodilla-tappers, who roamed the forests inland.

CANCÚN TO TULUM

Day One

Begin by exploring the more traditional side of **Cancún** *(p22)* with a *desayuno* (breakfast) at one of the Mercado 28 spots *(p93)*, in the town market. Then rent a car and drive south through the Hotel Zone along Boulevard Kukulcán.

Stop by the **Museo Maya de Cancún** *(p23)* and **El Rey** site *(p88)*, then head to **Playa Delfines** *(p89)* for surfing and great views.

Pause at **Puerto Morelos** *(p85)* for a lunch of seafood ceviche and a cool beer at Los Pelícanos *(p93)*, watching the pelicans hang in the breeze. After snorkeling over Puerto's reef, continue on to **Playa del Carmen** *(p26)*. Check out the beach and the shops on Quinta Avenida. As darkness falls, join the strolling crowds along the Quinta.

Day Two

After breakfast, continue south toward **Tulum** *(p32)*. Your route will take you past **Xplor** and **Xcaret**, as well as the glamorous vacation spot of **Puerto Aventuras** *(p95)*, and the gorgeous beaches of **Xpu-Ha** *(p97)* and **Akumal** *(p96)*. In Akumal, have lunch at **Tequilaville** *(p105)* before heading to Tulum to explore the cliff-top Maya site. Later, go for swimming and sunbathing on the beach, before enjoying dinner cooked over an open fire at **Hartwood** *(p105)*.

Maya ruins at the El Rey Site

The Best of the Rest

1. Playacar, Playa del Carmen

Q4

The plusher side of Playa del Carmen, with a fascinating jungle aviary in the midst of landscaped avenues lined with big resort hotels and private villas.

2. El Rey Site, Cancún

K5 Hotel Zone 9am–4:30pm daily

This was a relatively small Maya city, but its layout, with a clearly visible "main street," makes it easy to imagine people bustling about, buying and selling.

3. El Meco Site, Cancún

K2 Carretera Puerto Juarez, López Portillo 8am–4pm daily

The remains of an important Maya city, which was probably founded here in about 300 CE. They feature impressive carvings of animals and monsters.

4. Cenote Kantun-Chi, Playa del Carmen

P5 Carretera Federal Cancún-Tulum, km 1265 9am–5pm daily kantunchi.com

Visitors can enjoy a swim in the cenote's clear, freshwater pool. There's also a lovely underground cavern to explore.

5. Río Secreto, Playa del Carmen

Q4 Carretera Federal Libre Chetumal riosecreto.com

This underground cave features ancient rock formations that chronicle the planet's geological past.

6. Puerto Juárez and Punta Sam

K1–K2

The little passenger (Puerto Juárez) and car (Punta Sam) ferry ports for Isla Mujeres *(p30)* are older than any other part of Cancún.

7. Acamaya, Puerto Morelos

R3

A secluded spot ideal for getting away from just about everything, Acamaya is set at the end of the bumpy beach road north from Puerto Morelos. There's a small cabaña hotel and a camping site.

8. MUSA (Museo Subacuático de Arte)

K6 & L2 Blvd Kukulcán, km 15.3 9am–5pm daily musamexico.org

This subaquatic sculpture park is located across two offshore sites (Salon Machones and Salon Nizuc) between Cancún and Isla Mujeres.

9. Punta Maroma

R4

Among the palm-fringed bays at Punta Maroma are several reserved for guests at the luxurious Maroma retreat.

10. Moon Palace Cancún

R3 Carretera Cancún-Chetumal, km 36.5 moonpalace.com

One of the largest and best equipped of the Riviera's resorts, the Moon Palace is set in a secluded stretch of jungle to the south of Cancún.

Beaches

1. Playa Norte, Isla Mujeres

L1

A favorite spot for beach bums on Isla Mujeres, Playa Norte is a small but beautiful strip of white sand that offers plenty of options to stay entertained, from pedalos and kayaks to lively bars under the palms.

2. Playa Gaviota Azul, Cancún

L4 Blvd Kukulcán, km 9

One of the best beaches on the east side of town, Playa Gaviota Azul is located in the heart of the city's party scene *(p23)*. Come to join in the fun, then relax on the sands post-party.

3. Playa Delfines, Cancún

K5 Blvd Kukulcán, km 18

A great place to find space to stretch out, Playa Delfines has huge banks of white sand above pounding ocean surf. There's an amazing view north along the beachscape of Cancún Island.

4. Playa Secreto, Isla Mujeres

L1

Tucked away from the main North Beach, this broad, sheltered inlet is often uncrowded and the shallow waters here make it an ideal spot for families, especially those with little ones.

5. Isla Holbox

For lovers of real seclusion, Isla Holbox *(p85)* offers miles of beach from which visitors can pick the perfect spot to call their own. The island faces the opal waters of the Gulf of Mexico, however, so unlike much of the Riviera to the south, there's no coral.

6. Puerto Morelos

Excellent for carefree swimming, Puerto Morelos *(p85)* has not only fine, uncrowded white sands, but also a reef full of vivid underwater life just offshore.

7. Playa del Secreto

R4

A short way south of Puerto Morelos, this big, broad, white-sand beach is mostly fronted by private villas, with scarcely any hotels, so there's never any shortage of space.

8. Punta Bete

One of the most beautiful spots on the Riviera, Punta Bete *(p85)* features palms, white-sand bays, and turquoise sea. A terrible access road helps keep it that way.

9. Playa del Carmen

Playa del Carmen's *(p26)* main town beach is the place to go to join other sun worshipers, and to showcase your skills at beach volleyball and other seaside pursuits.

10. Chunzubul, Playa del Carmen

Q4

Keep walking along the beach north from Playa del Carmen to reach the town of Chunzubul. There are some great snorkeling and diving spots here, plus nudist beaches, if that appeals. It's best not to leave clothing unattended.

Fishing on Playa Secreto, Isla Mujeres

Places to Shop

1. La Casa del Arte Mexicano, Xcaret

K3 Km. 282 Carretera Chetumal-Puerto Juárez, Playa del Carmen

The gift shop at this folk-art museum, in Xcaret *(p28)*, stocks high-quality crafts from all over Mexico, including fun toys.

2. Forum by the Sea, Cancún

K4 Blvd Kukulcán, km 9.5

10am–midnight daily

Highlights here are perfume and jewelry stores and brands such as Harley Davidson and Zingara. It also has a huge Hard Rock Café at its center.

3. Coral Negro, Cancún

L4 Blvd Kukulcán, km 9.5

A rambling jewelry and handicrafts bazaar a few steps from the Forum. You can find fine traditional craftwork here, as well as a lot of junk.

4. Plaza Caracol, Cancún

K4 Blvd Kukulcán, km 8.5

One of the biggest and most varied of the Cancún malls, with engaging toy shops, beachwear, fine jewelry, and a huge choice of restaurants in an attractive, light-filled building.

Souvenirs for sale at a stall, Mercado 28

5. La Isla, Cancún

K4 Blvd Kukulcán, km 12.5

W islacancun.mx

One of the most stylish of the Hotel Zone's malls, built as an artificial island surrounded by Venetian-style "canals." It's the place for top names such as Hugo Boss, Diesel, and Zara.

6. Mercado 23, Cancún

J3 Off Av Tulum, on Calle Cedro

This colorful little open-air market is where locals go to shop for meat, vegetables, herbal cures, and many other items such as party supplies and piñatas.

7. Mercado 28, Cancún

J3 Av Xel-Ha and Av Tankah

The town market offers an old-style shopping experience, with stalls featuring a variety of items, including *huarache* sandals and panama hats, and tables full of fresh vegetables and fruits. There's a food court, too.

8. Avenida Hidalgo, Isla Town, Isla Mujeres

L1

This is Isla's main street, and its main drag for leisurely browsing. Here and in parallel Av Juárez small shops offer painted wooden birds, and local shell and coral jewelry.

9. Super Telas, Playa del Carmen

Q4 Constituyentes, Plaza Las Perlas

Fine-quality Mexican textiles *(telas)*, in traditional or original designs, can be found in this original shop.

10. Caracol, Playa del Carmen

Q4 Av 5, from Calle 6 to 84

The specialties at this two-story boutique are textiles and embroidery from all over Mexico – particularly Chiapas – and from Guatemala.

Clubs

Partygoers dancing at the Coco Bongo

1. Coco Bongo, Cancún

L4 Blvd Kukulcán, km 9.5 From 10:30pm daily cocobongo.com

Cancún's most high-powered, high-tech, multilevel mega-club, Coco Bongo has a wide range of music options.

2. Amma Club, Cancún

K4 Blvd Kukulcán, km 12.7 (998) 223 4656 9:30pm–3am Thu–Sat

In the steamy heat of the Yucatán, this ice bar has bartenders clad in ski goggles and anoraks, shaking up frosty cocktails as DJs spin a mix of reggaeton and house music.

3. Chicabal Sunset Club, Cancún

K5 Blvd Kukulcán, Marina del Rey 1–7pm Thu–Sun chicabalsunset.com

Situated on a private beach, this stylish club hosts pool parties and offers beautiful ocean views.

4. Captain Hook's Pirate Night, Cancún

K3 El Embarcadero, Blvd Kukulcán, km 4.5 Check in 6:30pm daily capitanhook.com

Dinner cruises are normally more sedate than clubbing in Cancún, but Captain Hook's Pirate Night, with its lively "pirate crew," tends to be quite boisterous.

5. La Casa del Hábano, Cancún

K4 Blvd Kukulcán, km 12.7 10am–9pm daily lacasadelhabano.com

With its wood-paneled walls and leather chairs, this place has a refined yet relaxed air. Along with selling a range of Cuban cigars, from Cohibas to Macanudos, the bar here serves up some of the best mojitos in town.

6. Cun Crawl, Cancún

L4 Blvd Kukulcán, km 9.5 (998) 165 0699

Chill out in the lounge area, or hit the dance floor, as the DJs mix and play creative blends of European music at this chic nightclub.

7. The City, Cancún

L4 Blvd Kukulcán, km 9.5 (998) 848 8385 (ext 115) Nightclub: 10pm–3am daily

This huge, modern nightclub also includes a beach club, restaurant, bar, and lounge. Note that sandals and bathing suits are not allowed.

8. Mandala, Playa del Carmen

H3 Calle 12 Av 10pm–4am daily mandalatickets.com

An Asian-inspired club, Mandala is massive, and fills up quickly on the weekends. Bottle service is available.

9. Coralina Daylight Club, Playa del Carmen

Q4 Calle 26 11am–7pm Tue–Sun coralinabeachclub.com

Coralina capitalizes on the Caribbean sun and sand and its enviable beach-side location to attract partygoers.

10. La Vaquita, Playa del Carmen

Q4 Calle 12 Norte (998) 848 8380 7pm–2am Tue–Sun

This lively nightclub, whose name means "Little Cow," is anything but pastoral, and has a man dressed as a cow, offering shots to the crowds.

Bars and Cafés

Colorful exterior of El Café Cito, Isla Mujeres

1. Hunter Bar, Cancún

J3 Alcatraces 45, Mz. 10, Lt. 26 SM 22, Centro 8am–3am daily

Enjoy cocktails and vegan food under the fairy lights at this bar. There's also karaoke on Wednesdays with a live band, welcome hammocks, and a pool.

2. Alux, Playa del Carmen

Q4 Av Juaréz 217 5:45–11pm daily

This restaurant-bar has an unusual setting: an atmospheric cave. It's a good spot for an evening drink or dinner. Later in the night, dance to DJs or live jazz.

3. Señor Frog's, Cancún

L4 Blvd Kukulcán, km 9.5 11am–2am daily

Beside Laguna Nichupté, this is one of the most popular Cancún outlets of the Anderson group. Party atmosphere, often with rock bands, guaranteed.

4. El Pabilo, Cancún

J3 Av Yaxchilán 31 7am–1pm daily

This cozy café, with a Bohemian feel, offers a welcome respite from loud nightclubs. Live music by local musicians and Cuban expats on weekends.

5. Lola Valentina, Isla Mujeres

L1 Av Miguel Hidalgo 7:30am–11:30pm daily

Enjoy breakfast smoothies and a cocktail menu featuring more than ten margaritas, including chipotle and *sriracha*. Only cash is accepted here.

6. El Café Cito, Isla Mujeres

L1 Av Juárez, corner of Av Matamoros, Isla Town 7:30am–2pm Tue–Sun

This mellow place, a few streets from the beach, offers excellent breakfasts and superior coffee, and fresh juice combos later in the day.

7. La Cueva del Chango Restaurante and Bar, Playa del Carmen

Q4 Calle 38 between 5ta Av and El Mar 8am–10:30pm daily (to 2pm Sun)

With its leafy patio, this place feels like a magical secret garden. House cocktails feature combinations such as the Manatí, which blends passionfruit, plantain, and basil with mezcal.

8. Rakata, Playa del Carmen

Q4 Calle 12 Norte 7pm–2am Fri–Sat

Urban Latin music and reggaeton dominate this club, which bills itself as Cancún's wildest. It also hosts occasional dance contests.

9. Pez Vela, Playa del Carmen

Q4 Av 5, by Calle 2 8am–11pm daily

A popular bar-restaurant with a terrace, this spot is a fixture on the Quinta Avenida promenade. The vibe is hippy-Caribbean, with reggae and rock bands.

10. Abolengo, Cancún

L4 Blvd Kulkulcán, km 9.5

This bar is known for its neon theme. Expect excellent food and a great cocktail menu along with diverse music.

Places to Eat

1. Le Chique, Puerto Morelos

R3 Puerto Morelos, km 27.5 karismahotels.com/lechique · $$$

With classic dishes, such as *cochinita pibil*, appealing to the palate and the eye, Le Chique is a perfect place to celebrate special occasions.

2. La Casa de los Mayoras, Cancún

J3 Calle Guadalupe Victoria and Miguel Hidalgo Donceles 28 (998) 256 8300 8am–5pm Mon–Sat · $

This vegetarian restaurant is famous for its breakfast, with every dish featuring locally sourced ingredients.

3. Ser Esencia, Isla Holbox

G1 Calle Igualdad, next to Sec Tec. 77310 casasandra.com/culinary · $$$

Located in the Ser Casasandra Hotel *(p130)*, this upscale restaurant is well worth a visit for its exceptional tasting menus and attentive service.

4. La Parrilla, Cancún

J3 Av Yaxchilán 51 laparrilla.com.mx · $$

With daily mariachi music creating a warm atmosphere, La Parrilla offers a good range of Mexican favorites such as grilled meats, soups, and fondues.

5. Mercado 28 Restaurants, Cancún

J3 Av Xel-Ha and Av Tankah · $

The courtyard of the town market is packed with canopied tables. The traditional food served, such as *pollo con mole*, is flavorful and affordable. Note, credit cards are not accepted.

6. North Garden, Isla Mujeres

L1 Carlos Lazo 14, Centro northgarden.com.mx · $$

The dishes here are based around locally farmed ingredients. Try the seafood canoe: baked pineapple stuffed with fish and seafood.

PRICE CATEGORIES

For a three-course meal for one with a beer or soda (or equivalent meal), taxes, and extra charges.

$ under US$15 $$ US$15–$35
$$$ over US$35

7. Los Pelícanos, Puerto Morelos

R3 On the Plaza · $$

Linger over the tasty seafood cocktails or the subtle fish dishes at this beach-terrace restaurant.

8. Lola Rooftop Restaurant, Playa del Carmen

Q4 Acceso Xcalacoco thefiveshotels.com.mx · $$

In the Fives Hotel, this restaurant serves Mediterranean-inspired dishes and offers stunning views.

9. Los Aguachiles, Playa del Carmen

Q4 Corner of Calle 34 and Av 25 · $

A low-key open-air snack joint, this place offers delicious tacos and tostadas and an even larger selection of salsas.

10. Las Brisas, Playa del Carmen

Q4 Carretera Federal Cancún · $$$

This big terrace-restaurant has a simple style, but its fresh local seafood is some of the best in town.

Plates of delicious grilled food at La Parrilla

COZUMEL AND THE SOUTH

The southern stretch of the Riviera offer something of a contrast to the north. It still has areas with luxury resorts and cultural attractions, but generally it's the less built-up part of the coast, with a slower pace of life and some truly untouched corners. Offshore, Cozumel is a relaxing island that offers fabulous diving opportunities. Onshore are some of the Caribbean's most dazzling tropical beaches, such as the seven bays of Xpu-Ha and the crescent of Media Luna Bay. They lead down the Caribbean coast to the great beach refuge of Tulum, with its world-famous Maya sites. A little way inland is another massive Maya site, the forest-clad city of Cobá.

For places to stay in this area, see p131

Distinctive lighthouse in San Miguel, Cozumel

1 Cozumel

Gleaming jewelry stores along the waterfront in San Miguel combine with an easygoing, small-town charm that has long made this island a favorite with families. Cozumel (*p24*) is a great place to settle into at a leisurely pace, maybe going diving one day, then exploring a little the next: around the island are Maya sites, windblown cliffs, a fascinating natural wildlife park at Punta Sur (*p63*), and lovely beaches and snorkeling spots on the west coast.

2 San Gervasio, Cozumel

R5 (998) 849 2885
8am–5pm daily

The remains of the Maya capital of Cozumel, seized by Cortés and his Spanish soldiers in 1519, are in the middle of the island. Its buildings are small compared to those of the great Maya cities, but there are many of them – and discovering them, through woods full of wonderful scents, flowers, and birds, involves a lovely walk.

3 Puerto Aventuras

Q5

Puerto Aventuras is the biggest, most opulent resort on the southern Riviera, a specially created vacation town around an inlet that's now a pretty pleasure port lined with shops and restaurants. The nine-hole golf course is attractive, and the marina is the best-equipped on the whole Riviera, making it a popular base for serious deep-sea fishing enthusiasts. You can take a dip in another part of the harbor.

4 Tulum

Home to a Maya city perched up on a cliff top, a 7-mile (11-km) palm-fringed beach, and an array of inventive restaurants and boutique hotels, Tulum (*p32*) is one of the region's most attractive destinations, particularly popular with independent travelers looking for a quieter spot than Playa or Cancún. There's good fishing and diving opportunities offshore, and the area around is dotted with beautiful cenotes to explore.

Colorful toucan in the lush Xel-Ha

5 Xel-Ha

P6 Carretera Chetumal, Puerto Juárez, km 240 8:30am–6pm daily xelha.com

One of the most luxuriant coral inlets on the coast has been made into a "snorkel park" that's one of the Riviera's most popular attractions – experienced divers may find it tame, but the easy snorkeling is great for families. Around it is a forest park and a beach. Just outside the park and across the highway is the Maya site of Xel-Ha *(p98)*.

6 Akumal

P5

Long a favorite dive destination, with fabulous reefs and places for cave diving, Akumal has grown a good deal without being overwhelmed. It spreads over several long, lovely bays – Media Luna is the most beautiful, with the delightful Yal-Ku lagoon *(p71)*. There are more apartments, villas, and small hotels than big developments. The beaches near Akumal village are favorite turtle breeding grounds.

7 The Cozumel Reefs

Cozumel's greatest glory is its 20-plus coral reefs, an awe-inspiring undersea world of caves, canyons, and coral "forests" teeming with life, from sea cucumbers and brilliantly luminous angelfish to graceful rays and the occasional shark. The water is almost perfectly clear and Chankanaab *(p61)* and Paraíso *(p25)* reefs are close, so can be appreciated even by inexperienced divers and snorkelers.

Swimming in a lagoon, Sian Ka'an Biosphere Reserve

8 Cobá

M5 8am–5pm daily inah.gob.mx

This huge Maya city was once home to around 50,000 people and was the great rival of Chichén Itzá *(p36)*. It's a very different place to visit – the remains of the city are spread out around several large lakes, and

THE SACBÉ OF COBÁ

Cobá was the center of the largest network of *sacbé* (or "white ways"), stone-paved roads, in the Maya world. They connected the various parts of the city, as well as linked it to vassal-cities. About 800 CE Cobá built the longest ever *sacbé*, of over 60 miles (100 km), to Yaxuná in the west, to help reinforce it in wars with Chichén Itzá – unsuccessfully, as Cobá was defeated shortly afterward.

to find its massive buildings you follow fascinating walks through a thick forest full of birds. Yucatán's tallest pyramid is here.

9 Xpu-Ha

P5

All along these seven gracefully sweeping bays, 2 miles (3 km) south of Puerto Aventuras, are some of the Riviera's most idyllic beaches, with exuberantly alive reefs and some of the most exquisite turquoise waters. Several are now occupied by resort complexes. However, two (signposted X-4 and X-7 from the highway) are still open to anyone, and at X-7 there are some small cabañas, a camping site, and a dive shop.

10 Sian Ka'an Biosphere Reserve

Mexico's largest wetland nature reserve, and a UNESCO World Heritage Site, Sian Ka'an *(p34)* brings the Riviera to an end just south of Tulum. Its vast area of virtually untouched mangroves, jungle, and beaches contains an extraordinary range of birds and wildlife, and the one-day tours run by local organizations give a glimpse of the surprising interplay of nature in this rare environment. The few inhabited spots along the coast are wonderful for fishing, and have a feel of tranquil isolation.

COZUMEL IN A DAY

Morning

Start with breakfast at **Las Palmeras** *(p104)*, watching the new arrivals off the Playa del Carmen ferry. Browse in the jewelry and souvenir shops along the waterfront and in the streets around the square. Rent a car and head out of town down Avenida Juárez to the Maya site of **San Gervasio** *(p95)*. If you hire a guide at the entrance, don't let them hurry you, but take time to notice the birds and vegetation – as much of an attraction as the site. Back at the main road, head left to meet the east coast at windswept **Punta Santa Cecilia** *(p24)*. Turn south down the road beside the rocks and waves for lunch at **Chen Río** *(p105)*.

Afternoon

Carry on down the coast to **Punta Sur Eco Beach Park** *(p63)*. From the parking lot, walk down to Punta Celaraín lighthouse and the strange little Maya temple called the Caracol, and follow the nature trail to see some crocodiles and flamingos.

You can snorkel at Punta Sur, but you'll see more marine life if you continue on to **Laguna Chankanaab** *(p24)*. If all you want is a placid beach, stop at **Playa San Francisco** *(p103)*. Drive back to town, and don't miss the sunset from the Malecón waterfront.

Swimmers in the pool of the Gran Cenote

The Best of the Rest

1. Paamul

Q5

Paamul is a favorite destination of RV travelers from the US and Canada, who take advantage of generous long-term rates to settle in for the whole winter. The campsite also has cabañas, a beach bar *(p103)*, and a dive shop, which caters for the keen divers who come here to explore the offshore dive sites.

2. Tankah

P6

Off the beaten track, Tankah is a placid, narrow beach with a fine reef, a restaurant, and a small cluster of villas and hotels. Behind the beach, by the Casa Cenote restaurant, there's a broad, reed-lined cenote, so it's a toss-up between swimming in the surf or the perfectly still freshwater pool.

3. Xel-Ha Site

P6 8:30am–7pm daily

Across the highway from the popular snorkel park *(p96)* is this little-visited Maya city, one of the oldest in the region. Archaeologists reckon the settlement originated around 100 BCE but only became a prominent city during the Classic Period *(p8)*. Today, the city contains several well-preserved stone buildings and temples, along with two cenotes. On some buildings there are beautiful frescoes, some of which date back to about 200 CE.

4. Gran Cenote

N6 8am–4:45pm daily

The Cobá road north from Tulum is one of the best places to find swimmable cenotes, and this is one of the best. It's made up of several caverns, filled with some of the clearest waters you're likely to see. As such, it's become a must for swimmers and snorkelers who come to spot small fish and turtles.

5. Aktun-Ha Cenote

N6 8am–4:45pm daily

Located outside of Tulum is this fine swimming-hole cenote, which is also known as Cenote Carwash. The shallow depth of the cave (40 ft/13 m) makes it ideal for entry-level divers to practice with a guide before venturing into open waters. Swimmers and snorkelers can also explore the huge main cavern.

6. Dos Ojos Cenote

P6 8am–5pm daily cenotedosojos.com

Between Playa del Carmen and Tulum is this cenote, which is very possibly the world's longest underwater cave system. The caves stretch for 220 miles (350 km) and include the deepest passage in Quintana Roo at 396 ft (118 m). The water is incredibly clear and the snorkeling or diving tours run by local tour operators are a memorable experience, with suitable tours for all abilities.

7. Aktun-Chen Cave

P5 9:30am–5:30pm daily aktun-chenpark.com

Located in thick jungle is this giant cave, considered one of the best caves to visit in the world. It's said to be over five million years old and contains a series of chambers and stalagmite towers, plus an underground river. A well-lit path leads through this beautiful subterranean world.

8. Muyil Site

G4 8am–5pm daily

The location is the attraction of this old, atmospheric Maya city set in hot, steamy jungle between the Highway and Lake Chunyaxché, in the Sian Ka'an reserve *(p34)*. Its proximity to the Muyil lagoon meant it was a key trading port during the Maya time and it remained occupied until the Spanish arrival. Only part of the site has been excavated so far, but this includes the 57-ft- (17-m-) high Castillo, which is the tallest pyramid in the Riviera Maya.

9. Punta Laguna

N4 7am–5pm daily puntalagunamx.com

Set in a tiny village by a forest lake north of Cobá, this nature reserve is one of the best places to see spider monkeys in the Yucatán. The park contains a substantial population of monkeys (both spider and howler varieties), along with a wide variety of tropical birds and plant species. Tours are offered throughout the day, with villagers as guides.

10. Road from Boca Paila to Punta Allen

G4–5

This journey is one for the adventurous. It follows a mostly unpaved road that is among the most bumpy, rutted, overgrown, and deserted roads in the whole of the Yucatán. The upshot is that you will enjoy great vistas of sea and forest, and may spot wildlife, including crocodiles, iguanas, and pelicans, along the way. If you want to drive this route, do so in a four-wheel drive vehicle.

A spider monkey spotted in Punta Laguna

Water lilies in Aktun-Ha cenote

Places to Shop

Punta Langosta shopping complex, Cozumel

1. Azul Gallery, Cozumel

R5 449 Av 15 Norte, between Calle 8 and Calle 10, San Miguel

At this quaint art gallery, watch American artist Greg Dietrich engrave blown glass to create unique vessels and lamps. The gallery also features paintings, jewelry, and other items made by local artists.

2. Punta Langosta, Cozumel

R5

This leisure mall, set in the cruise terminal, has major international fashion names plus upscale handicrafts and glittering gem stores.

3. Josa, Tulum

P6 Carretera Boca Paila, km 1.5, Quintana Roo, Tulum
(984) 115 8441

Inspired by the tropical and relaxed vibe of the Tulum beaches, this chic boutique sells fashionable accessories and clothing for women.

4. Tulum Bazaar, Tulum

P6 Av Tulum

An amazing hotchpotch of stores in true Mexican flea-market style. Souvenirs, Maya handicrafts, textiles, and jewelry abound. Be ready to haggle for the best deals.

5. Los Cinco Soles, Cozumel

R5 Av Rafael Melgar 27, by Calle 8, San Miguel

This Malecón handicrafts store is the place to do all your souvenir shopping in one go – clothes, tablecloths, jewelry, glassware, metal or papier-mâché birds and animals, and more.

6. Unicornio, Cozumel

R5 Av 5 Sur, near Calle 1 Sur, San Miguel

A big, varied crafts dealer, with especially good ceramics and painted wood. There's junk as well as quality pieces, but it's a great place to browse.

7. Shalom, Tulum

P6 Av Tulum, between Calle Orion and Calle Centauro

Get dressed for a Tulum-style beach party at this cool shop selling hippy-style clothing plus sleeker items that you could wear when out clubbing.

8. Pro Dive, Cozumel

R5 Adolfo Rosado Salas 198, corner of Av 5, San Miguel

First port of call for self-sufficient sea-explorers, with every possible kind of diving and snorkeling gear.

9. Puerto Aventuras

Q5

A small, stylish group of shops. Among the cigars and sophisticated jewelry, you'll also find Mexican designer clothing at Arte Maya and fine handicrafts at El Guerrero.

10. Mixik Artesanías, Tulum

P6 Av Tulum, opposite the bus terminal

This charming store is a treasure trove for visitors looking to immerse themselves in Tulum's local culture. It offers a high-quality collection of colorful craftwork from all across the country.

Beaches

1. Playa San Francisco and Playa Sol, Cozumel

R5–R6

These are two of the many great beaches on Cozumel's southwest coast: San Francisco and others near it are good for relaxation; Sol is best if you want a beach with lots going on.

2. South Beach, Tulum

P6

The place for people who want to find some seclusion in Tulum, with longer, broader, whiter beaches, acres of space, and quite luxurious comforts in some cabañas.

3. Media Luna Bay, Akumal

P5

"Half Moon Bay" is an exquisite crescent of brilliant white sand and calm sea. The atmosphere is just as tranquil: around it there are condos and villas; at the north end is the lovely Yal-Ku *(p71)* lagoon.

4. Xcacel Beach

P6 Xcacel 504

Lined by lush forest on one side and ocean on the other, the white-sand Xcacel Beach brims with natural beauty. It's also one of the places that help conservation efforts to protect endangered sea turtles.

5. Xpu-Ha

Seven bays *(p97)* with some of the coolest, whitest sand and most colorful coral on the Riviera. Several are occupied by resorts, but X-4 and X-7 are open to anyone.

6. Chen Río, Cozumel

R5

This is the best beach located on Cozumel's rugged eastern shore, with a sheltered cove for swimming and surfing farther along. There's a great beach restaurant worth a special visit.

7. Playa Akumal

P5

A bustling beach in the center of Akumal *(p96)*; behind it there's a good choice of low-key bars and shops.

8. North Beach, Tulum

P6

The beaches at the north end of Tulum *(p32)* are great if you want to hang out and meet people in the inexpensive cabañas. They also have the best view of the Maya site.

9. Punta Xamach and Conoco

G5

Getting to these remote, deserted beaches involves negotiating the wild, rutted road between Boca Paila and Punta Allen *(p99)*.

10. Bahía Punta Solimán, Tulum

P6

Shaded by palms, this near-empty beach feels remote, even though it's only down a dirt track from the highway. A few boats and a bar are the main signs of habitation.

Kayaks on the palm-fringed beach, Bahía Punta Solimán

Nightspots

1. Al Cielo, Puerto Aventuras
Q5 Xpu-Ha Beach 11:30am–9pm daily
The exclusive Al Cielo offers guests one-of-a-kind events on Xpu-Ha Beach, often with the moon-lit ocean as a backdrop. It features top-class musicians, dancers, and other entertainment.

2. La Internacional Cervecería, Cozumel
R5 Av Rafael Melgar, by 7 Sur and 11 Sur, San Miguel (987) 869 1289
With a focus on beers, this bar offers a fine selection of international and Mexican brews, specially sourced from craft brewers around the country.

3. Plaza del Sol, Cozumel
R5 Melgar at Av Juárez, San Miguel
Cozumel doesn't have a particularly wild nightlife. Instead, San Miguel's central plaza is the best place to be – especially on Sundays, when there's usually live music.

4. La Zebra, Tulum
G4 Beach Rd, km 4.6
La Zebra's Sunday-night salsa party draws people from up and down the beach as well as from town. Come early for the free dance classes.

5. Hard Rock Café, Cozumel
R5 Av Rafael Melgar 2A, San Miguel From 10pm daily
The Maya-style architecture of the building makes it a stunning location for the rock memorabilia chain. There's also occasional live music.

6. Las Palmeras, Cozumel
R5 Av Rafael Melgar 1, Centro 7am–10pm daily (987) 872 0532
This friendly Caribbean hut of a bar is set opposite the ferry landing on San Miguel's plaza. It is great for drinks, and it does highly enjoyable breakfasts.

Entrance to Carlos 'n Charlie's in Cozumel

7. Joel's Bar, Puerto Aventuras
Q5 On the Marina 4pm–1am daily
Enjoy a wide range of entertainment, such as live music performances, preceded or accompanied by dinner at this amazing bar.

8. Carlos 'n Charlie's, Cozumel
R5 Av Rafael Melgar 551, San Miguel From 11am daily
Cozumel's biggest bar, restaurant, and music venue is the place where you're assured of finding a (usually pretty raucous) crowd every night, partying in the open air to classic rock circa 1970 to present.

9. Kin Toh, Tulum
P6 Carretera Tulum-Punta Allen, km 5
Treetop hangouts called "nests" overlooking the jungle are a famous feature of Kin Toh. Cocktails have local spirits and ingredients, such as *xtabentún*, a Yucatecan liqueur made with honey and notes of anise.

10. Mezzanine, Tulum
P6 Carretera Boca Paila, km 1.5 From 11am daily
This stylish restaurant-bar combines luxurious indulgence with eco-friendly policies. Sip one of their signature cocktails while enjoying the beats from guest DJs.

Places to Eat

1. Guido's, Cozumel

R5 Av Rafael Melgar 23, between Calle 6 and Calle 8, San Miguel (987) 872 0946 · $$$

Known for its rich lasagne, Guido's serves great Italian food. Enjoy your food outside in the garden.

2. Rock'n Java, Cozumel

R5 Av Rafael Melgar 602, between Calle 7 and Av Quintana Roo, San Miguel (987) 872 4405 · $$

The big fresh salads and sandwiches are great at this American-run café on the water. Save some room for a huge slice of apple pie or one of the other gooey desserts.

3. Casa Denis, Cozumel

R5 Calle 1 Sur, San Miguel From 7am daily · $$

One of the island's oldest venues, Casa Denis serves classic Yucatecan dishes *(p74)* at low prices.

4. Arca Tulum

P6 Av Tulum-Boca Paila, km 7.6 L & Mon arcatulum.com· $$$

"From fire to table" is the motto of this restaurant, where the menu changes regularly. Seasonal and locally-sourced produce is prepared by a chef who has worked in the world's top restaurants.

5. La Cocay, Cozumel

R5 Calle 8, between Av 10 and Av 15, San Miguel · $$$

Set in a Caribbean-style wooden hut, this mellow place offers a range of Mediterranean-inspired dishes.

6. La Palapa de Marlon, Puerto Aventuras

Q5 Calzada Puerto Maya, Lote 5 9am–5pm Mon, noon–7:30pm Tue–Sun · $

Try some of the region's best seafood here. Dishes include shrimp, fish, and octopus tacos, and nine different types of ceviche.

PRICE CATEGORIES

For a three-course meal for one with a beer or soda (or equivalent meal), taxes, and extra charges.

$ under US$15 **$$** US$15–$35 **$$$** over US$35

7. Tequilaville, Akumal

P5 Calle Principal (984) 875 9022 · $$

This small restaurant serves a pleasant selection of traditional Mexican food and, allegedly, the best hamburger in the Riviera Maya.

8. Cetli, Tulum

P6 Calle Polar at Calle Orion (984) 108 0681 · $$

A Mexico City-trained chef-owner turns out light, refined versions of Mexican classics such as *chiles en nogada* (stuffed chilies with walnut sauce) at Cetli.

9. Hartwood, Tulum

P6 Tulum Beach Rd, km 7.6 · $$$

Across from the beach and set in lush jungle. Hartwood's chefs cook over an open fire and produce top-class cuisine. Reservations are strongly suggested.

10. Chen Río, Cozumel

R5 Chen Río Beach · $$

The best restaurant on Cozumel's east coast, and a wonderful place to eat on the beach.

Patrons dining outside of Casa Denis

THE CENTRAL HEARTLAND

Away from the party hot spots and nature preserves along the Caribbean coast is the vast and varied interior of the Yucatán, an area of low hills, giant sinkholes, and cenote pools perfect for swimming. This is the region where the ancient Maya people built some of their greatest creations, in Ek-Balam and the magnificent city of Chichén Itzá, which may be the most famous site in the whole of Mexico. Elsewhere, there are numerous Spanish-founded towns to explore, such as Valladolid or Tizimín, many of which have retained the colorful buildings, churches, and vast plazas that were constructed during this era. It's in these places that you'll find a gently paced street life along with an unmistakable Yucatecan identity and sense of culture, with Maya people selling their handcrafted wares.

For places to stay in this area, see p132

1 Balankanché Caves

E3 8am–5pm daily

This great labyrinthine complex of caves extends for miles under the Yucatán forest. Caves were sacred for the ancient Maya and, in one spectacular chamber, the sanctuary, remains were found of over 100 ritual incense burners. The compulsory tour ends in a magical chamber with a perfectly still pool, in which the cave bottom seen through the water is a mirror image of the roof.

2 Dzitnup and Samula Cenotes

E3 Dzitnup village 8am–5pm daily

Easily accessible from Valladolid, these two spectacular swimmable cenotes are among some of the greatest sights of the Yucatán.

Vast underground cavern at Dzitnup Cenote

Dzitnup can be entered through a cramped tunnel, which emerges into a vast, cathedral-like cavern, pierced by a shaft of sunlight and filled with tower-shaped rocks. Only a five-minute walk away, Samula is a large, shallow pool of crystal-clear water, into which the roots of an aged tree dangle through a crack in the rocky ceiling.

3 San Felipe

E1

To the west of Río Lagartos *(p108)*, this village is smaller and has a superb, usually near-empty beach on the sandbar across the lagoon, facing the opal waters of the Gulf of Mexico. Village boatmen will ferry you to and from the beach, and also offer flamingo tours. You can see fabulous sunsets from the village.

4 Aké

C2 8am–5pm daily

inah.gob.mx

This city west of Izamal is a mystery, as its drum-shaped columns and ramp-like stairways are quite unlike other Maya buildings. The local church was built on an ancient Maya pyramid. Alongside the site is a 19th-century henequen hacienda, San Lorenzo de Aké, filled with vintage machinery.

5 Ek-Balam

E2 8am–5pm daily inah.gob.mx

In 1998, excavations revealed some of the finest examples of Maya sculpture here, on the giant temple-mound known as the Acropolis. Most spectacular is El Trono (The Throne), a temple entrance believed to be the tomb of Ukit-Kan-Lek-Tok, who ruled around 800 CE. Nearby is an intricate mass of finely carved figures. The rest of the Acropolis is a multilevel palace.

6 Río Lagartos

F1

This quiet village on the remote north coast is at the head of over 12 miles (20 km) of mangrove lagoon and mudflats, with the Yucatán's largest colonies of flamingos and a dazzling variety of other birds.

7 Chichén Itzá

Chichén Itzá is the most famous and awe-inspiring of the great Maya cities *(p36)*. The pyramid of El Castillo, the Ball Court, the Sacred Cenote, and the Temple of the Warriors are must-sees, while many sites also feature spine-tingling images of war and sacrifice.

Striking San Antonio monastery in Izamal

8 Valladolid

E3 San Bernardino: Parque de San Bernardino 9am–8pm Wed–Mon

Founded in 1545, the Spanish capital of the eastern Yucatán has one of the region's most iconic colonial plazas, overlooked by a towering white cathedral. Valladolid is famed for embroidery, and the square is a good place to buy traditional white flower-patterned *huípiles* (blouses) and tablecloths. Around the city are many fine old Spanish churches and houses, including the 17th-century townhouse, Casa de los Venados, housing a great collection of contemporary Mexican folk art. Four blocks from the plaza you can look down into the pit of Cenote Zací, once Valladolid's main water source. Close by is San Bernardino de Siena *(p52)*. Begun in 1552, it is the oldest permanent church in the Yucatán, with a gallery of graceful arches along the facade and a cloister of giant, squat stone columns set around a garden. Inside are some rare 18th-century Baroque altars and altarpieces.

9 Izamal

D2

The most unaltered Spanish-era city in the Yucatán, known as *Ciudad Dorada* or "Golden City" for the color of its buildings, is centered on the huge San Antonio monastery *(p52)*, begun in 1549, and the shrine of Our Lady of Izamal, the region's patron saint. Nearby are the remains of three pyramids, traces of a much older Maya city.

10 Telchac and Uaymitún

C2

Far west of San Felipe, a road runs along the coast through quiet fishing villages. Seaward, there are endless, often empty, beaches; on the landward side is a lagoon full of birds. Telchac is a fishing harbor with fine beaches and a few cheap hotels and low-key restaurants. At Uaymitún *(p63)* there is a free observation tower for bird-watching in the lagoon.

THE SALT OF CHICHÉN

Salt was one of the greatest sources of wealth in ancient America. In the lagoons near Río Lagartos there are huge salt flats, which are still in operation. Around 800 CE, Chichén Itzá won control of them and built its own port at El Cerritos, east of Río Lagartos, to trade in salt. The wealth this gave Chichén Itzá was a major reason why it dominated the Yucatán.

A TWO-DAY TOUR

Day One

Stay the night in **Valladolid**, or the little town of Pisté (close to Chichén Itzá), or better still one of the hotels just outside the site, such as Hacienda Chichén *(p132)*. Arrive at the **Chichén Itzá** (p36) early to beat the crowds. You'll need at least three hours for exploring the site, before lunch at Las Mestizas in **Pisté** *(p113)*.

In the afternoon, go up to **Ek-Balam**, or head into Valladolid for a wander around its plaza, San Bernardino church *(p52)*, and the dramatic town cenote. Before the day ends, head north to **Río Lagartos** *(p108)* (65 miles/105 km) to reserve a flamingo tour for the next morning. Stay at the Hotel San Felipe in **San Felipe** *(p107)*.

Day Two

The flamingos are best seen early, so start at around 7am. A two- or four-hour tour takes you into an exuberant, rare natural world, through broad lagoons and narrow creeks. Afterward, for lunch, have ceviche at Restaurante Vaselina on the waterfront, or head to **Tizimín** *(p110)* for locally sourced seafood at **Casa Makech** *(p113)*. From Tizimín, turn westward to reach **Izamal**. Here you can look out on the city from the monastery's arcaded courtyard. Its golden colors are especially lovely in the early evening light.

The Best of the Rest

1. Ik Kil Cenote

E3 Highway 180, 2 miles (3 km) E of Chichén Itzá 8am–5pm daily

A huge, circular pit filled with a beautiful underground pool – now the center of a private nature park.

2. Yaxcabá

D3

Set in the woods, this tranquil little town surprises with its 18th-century church, which features a three-tower facade and a wooden altarpiece.

3. Calotmul

E2

Between Valladolid and Tizimín, this country town has a fine 18th-century church with a Baroque altarpiece.

4. Tizimín

E2

The hub of Yucatán's "cattle country" is a non-touristy market town. At its center are two spacious squares, divided by two Spanish monasteries.

5. El Cuyo

F1

Visitors can enjoy miles of Gulf coast near this tiny fishing village.

Historic Iglesia de Santo Nino Jesus, Tihosuco

6. Tihosuco

E4

Located 30 miles (48 km) south of Valladolid, this remote village was where the Maya revolt of the Caste War began.

7. Bocas de Dzilam

D1

This vast area of mangroves west of San Felipe is remote and wild. There are no regular tours.

8. El Bajo

D1

Alongside the north coast road is a long, narrow sand-spit island, El Bajo, with coconut-palm shaded beaches.

9. Xcambó

C2 (999) 913 4034 8am–5pm daily

The atmospheric site of a coastal Maya town, probably an outlying Dzibilchaltún settlement, with great views from the top of its pyramid.

10. Cenote Yokdzonot

D3 Yokdzonot village, 9 miles (14 km) West of Pisté 9am–6pm daily

The little-visited village of Yokdzonot, a short drive from Pisté and Chichén Itzá, is home to a delightful, vine-clad cenote, perfect for an afternoon dip. Life jackets and snorkeling gear are available.

Shops and Markets

Ancient Maya stone calendar, Chichén Itzá

1. Main Plaza, Valladolid

E3

Maya women from the surrounding villages display their beautifully bright *huípiles* and other embroidery on the railings of the Parque Principal.

2. Coqui Coqui Perfumeria, Valladolid

E3 Calle 41A, 207A
coquicoqui.com

The Valladolid branch of this small perfumery chain offers a wide range of scents, all made from locally sourced ingredients. It also specializes in creating personalized fragrances.

3. Handicrafts Market, Chichén Itzá

E3

Around the Chichén Itzá visitor center there is something approaching a mall of handicrafts stalls, some of which are run by Maya selling their own embroidery, hammocks, and wood carvings.

4. Kaxtik Arte Mexicano, Valladolid

E3 Calle 41, 204 (985) 856 1969

Located in the center of the city, this charming store sells a wide variety of products ranging from high-quality clothes to locally made handcrafted items.

5. Raíces Mayas, Izamal

D2 Calle 30, 296, between Calle 29 and 31, Col. Centro

In the colorful area of Izamal known as Pueblo Magico, is this small store filled with artisanal crafts and decorative items for the home, all made in the on-site workshop.

6. Valladolid Crafts Market and Bazaar

E3 Mercado de Artesanías Calle 39, corner of Calle 44

Valladolid's semi-official handicrafts market has some fine embroidery, as well as more mass-produced goods. The nearby bazaar has a quirky set of shops around a food court.

7. Market, Tizimín

E2 Calle 47, 394 A
8am–5pm daily

Not a place for souvenirs but a real, bustling country-town market, with great fruit and other produce, and household goods.

8. Yalat, Valladolid

E3 Corner of Calle 39 and Calle 40

Set on Valladolid's central plaza, Yalat offers jewelry, embroidered clothes, chocolate, and sisal-fiber bath scrubs.

9. Hecho a Mano, Izamal

D2 Calle 31A, 308 sanmiguelhotel.com.mx/hotel/handicrafts

In the San Miguel hotel is this pretty little shop with a more carefully selected display of hand-made folk art than in the markets, as well as striking photographs of Yucatecan scenes and traditional crafts made by local artisans.

10. Market, Izamal

D2 Calle 31/Calle 32

Izamal's market, just below the monastery, has an attractive range of souvenirs, handicrafts, and busy little cafés.

Bars and Cafés

Traditional palapas at Pueblo Maya, Pisté

1. Absenta Pub, Valladolid

E3 Parque Flamboyanes (985) 856 0763 6pm–2am daily

This popular watering hole is known for chicken wings, burgers, and fried mozzarella sticks, as well as its live music and attentive servers.

2. El Yuktko Cantina Bar, Valladolid

E3 Calle 46, 236A (985) 110 8178

El Yuktko offers a wide variety of beers paired with a menu of tapas favorites. With its relaxed and fun atmosphere, it's the perfect place to unwind after a day of exploring the city.

3. Hacienda Chichén, Chichén Itzá

E3 Hotel Zone

This historic ranch-hotel *(p132)*, on the fringes of the Chichén Itzá site, has a terrace restaurant-bar perfect for a cocktail after a day of exploration.

4. Mezcaleria Don Trejo, Valladolid

E3 Calzada de Los Frailes (985) 688 0833

Located in the city center, this bar is the go-to place for mezcal, offering a wide range of traditional Mexican varieties. Live music performances and DJ sets are an added draw.

5. Soletana Café Santuario, Valladolid

E3 Calzada de Los Frailes 209 (985) 130 0069 8am–10:30pm daily

Located inside the Verde Morada hotel *(verdemorada.mx)*, this café serves pour-over coffee and drinks inspired by local ingredients.

6. Pueblo Maya, Pisté

E3 Calle 15, 48B, Manzana No. 13

Enjoy tasty Mexican food at Pueblo Maya, which is also a craft market. It has a lovely pool and hammocks to lounge in after your meal.

7. Anahata Café and Bistro, El Cuyo

F1 Av Veraniega, Calle 17, 142 7:30am–1pm daily

This café serves a wide variety of coffees, including an unusual pink latte. Try its other offbeat items like avocado toast with *chapulínes* (grasshoppers).

8. Elela Organic Vegan Café, Valladolid

E3 Calle 45 between 45 and 54a Colonial Sisal (984) 133 9265

Popular local café Elela is known for its unique creations and sesame-based menu, which includes tacos, tamales, and halva lattes – all made with produce grown in the on-site garden.

9. Market Bars, Izamal

D2 Calle 31, by Calle 32

Several cafés and *loncherías* here share a terrace, a fine vantage point on the monastery and city life. Some serve beer; some only soft drinks with snacks.

10. Kanché, Izamal

D2 Calle 28, 293

Izamal may not be known for its nightlife, but this spot is an exception. Expect innovative cocktails featuring nice additional touches like salt rims with begonia and corn essence.

Places to Eat

1. Restaurante Zací, Valladolid

E3 Calle 37 (985) 856 0721 · $

Hearty portions of local specialties are served under a *palapa* here, all with a view of the Cenote Zací. You can even take a dip before or after your meal.

2. Cocinas Económicas, Valladolid

E3 Calle 39, on Parque Principal · $

Around the bazaar on the square there's a line of self-service food counters. Noisy, with lots of atmosphere, this is a great place for a good breakfast, and to try out local snacks.

3. Casa Italia, Valladolid

E3 Calle 35, 202 · $

Overlooking a quaint plaza a short walk from the city center, this family-run restaurant serves the best Italian food in Valladolid, drawing a loyal crowd of locals and visitors. The thin-crust pizzas and pasta dishes are delicious.

4. Chaya's Natural Café, Ek-Balam

E2 Off the NE corner of the town plaza · $$

The restaurant at Genesis Retreat is open to non-guests only in the afternoon, but the crêpes and chocolate-chili cookies make it well worth a visit.

5. Las Mestizas, Pisté

E3 (985) 851 0069 · $$

The prettiest of the restaurants along the main road in Pisté, with charming service. It dishes up a delicious *sopa de lima (p75)*.

6. Hostería del Marqués, Valladolid

E3 Calle 39, on Parque Principal (985) 856 3042 · $$

Valladolid's best hotel also has its most eminent restaurant, with tables around a plant-filled patio. Its versions of local specialties like *lomitos de Valladolid* are definitive.

PRICE CATEGORIES

For a three-course meal for one with a beer or soda (or equivalent meal), taxes, and extra charges.

$ under US$15 $$ US$15–$35
$$$ over US$35

7. Casa Makech, Tizimín

E2 Calle 51, 403 (986) 113 7131 · $

This spot uses fresh, local ingredients to create dishes like octopus marinated in *achiote*, bitter orange, and sweet chili. Ask for a seat in the shady garden.

8. Yerba Buena del Sisal, Valladolid

E3 Calle 54A, 217 (985) 856 1406 · $

This charming restaurant is decorated with *papel picado* banners and is a great option for vegetarians.

9. Restaurante Vaselina, San Felipe

E1 (986) 862 2083 · $$

A big, unfussy place on the seafront where you can try wonderfully fresh, fat shrimp, octopus, and conch.

10. Kinich, Izamal

D2 Calle 27, 299, between Calle 28 and Calle 30 (988) 954 0489 D · $$

Set in a lush garden, this place has a high reputation for classic Yucatecan food, such as *poc-chuc (p74)*.

Dining at the Hostería del Marqués, Valladolid

THE WEST

Nowhere is the flavor of the Yucatán more pronounced than in the west of the region, around its historic capital, Mérida. In these parts, there is an extraordinary density of Maya relics and, although they may not match the awe-inspiring power of Chichén Itzá, sites such as Uxmal show the architecture of the Maya at its most elegant. Beyond the main sights are stretches of wilderness, hidden lagoons, and small towns covered with bougainvillea and hibiscus.

For places to stay in this area, see p132

1 Labná

C4 8am–5pm daily

The Arch of Labná, wonderfully drawn by Frederick Catherwood, exemplifies the sophistication of Puuc architecture. Nearby, the town's Palacio is only slightly smaller than Sayil's, and was divided into seven patios – the part to the left (west) was home to the lords of Labná, while the patios to the right were for servants. The setting, in tranquil woods full of birds, is especially lovely.

2 Uxmal

With the elegant lines of the Nunnery Quadrangle and towering mass of the Pyramid of the Magician, Uxmal *(p42)* is not only one of the most beautiful of ancient Maya cities but also one of the greatest sights in the Yucatán.

3 Celestún

A3

Just north of this fishing village is a silent, watery expanse of mangrove lagoon that is a breeding ground for flamingos, ibises, egrets, and blue herons. Boat tours are very popular (the lagoon can get rather crowded at times). Stay over in Celestún after the tours have gone back to Mérida to enjoy this tranquil village, with its white beach, laid-back restaurants and hotels, and fabulous sunsets.

Flamingos wading through the water, Celestún

4 Campeche

This Spanish-era walled city *(p46)* retains a charming old-world feel. The 17th-century ramparts and bastions were built to defend it against pirates. The streets within are lined with delicately colored old houses featuring patios and iron-grilled windows. A museum, housed in an old Spanish fort, contains jade funeral masks and other fine relics from the excavated site at Calakmul.

Vintage streetcars on the plaza, Campeche

TREN MAYA

In December 2024, Mexico launched the *Tren Maya (p124)*, an ambitious tourism project aimed at improving connectivity and access across the region. However, it has faced serious criticism over its social and environmental impacts. Construction of the line necessitated mass deforestation and destruction of local ecosystems. Alongside this, many historical sites have been put at risk and Maya people have lost their lands.

5 Dzibilchaltún

C2

The Temple of the Seven Dolls, through which the sun strikes at dawn on spring and fall equinoxes to run straight along a white *sacbé* (rough-cast road) to the central plaza, is the most celebrated feature of this Maya city just north of Mérida. It was one of the longest-inhabited Maya cities, occupied for over 2,000 years. There are additional temples at the site, as well as a grand Palacio and a Spanish missionary chapel. The huge pool, Cenote Xlacah (open 8am–5pm daily), which provided the ancient city with water, now offers an idyllic place in which to cool off. Admission is free on Sundays.

6 Kabah

C4 8am–5pm daily

This was the second most important of the Puuc cities *(p45)* after Uxmal, and an imposing arch on its west side marks the start of the *sacbé* road *(p96)* that linked it to its larger ally. Its Codz Poop, or "Palace of Masks," is the most extravagant example of Maya carving: the facade is covered with 250 faces of the long-nosed rain god Chac.

7 Sayil

C4 8am–5pm daily

Of all the Puuc cities, Sayil is the one that gives the strongest sense of the huge wealth of its ancient inhabitants. Its hub is the magnificent Palacio, a complex that sweeps up through three levels and more than 90 chambers, with an architectural refinement that recalls the buildings of ancient Greece. It housed over 350 people and had its own exclusive water supply.

8 Mérida

Mérida *(p40)* is perhaps the most appealing of all the colonial cities in Mexico, with elegant architecture, shady patios, great markets, and a distinct friendliness. With the soft music of *boleros* and the *jarana* heard in free concerts in 16th-century squares, and fiestas enjoyed by all ages every Sunday, the city's appeal is plentiful and varied.

Beach with the pier in the backdrop, Progreso

9 Progreso
C2

Mérida's port and favorite beach town is a place to get close to ordinary Yucatecan life. The harbor is set at the end of a 4-mile (6-km) pier, and the shallow waters around the beach remain blissfully tranquil. It's calm until the weekend, that is, when Meridanos spill out onto the sand and into the warm blue waters. There are excellent fish restaurants along the seafront, too, with large, convivial outside terraces on which to socialize.

10 Loltún Caves
C4 For tours: 9:30am–4pm daily

This vast cave complex is both a stunning natural phenomenon and an ancient Maya site. It has been occupied by humans longer than anywhere else in the Yucatán, from remote prehistory right up until the 19th century. The ancient Maya lived here, mined the caves, and used them for rituals. Guided tours take visitors through 1.5 miles (2 km) of caves, but the network extends much further. The rock formations are awe-inspiring, and a special feature of Loltún is its strange changes of temperature, from fierce heat to chilly breezes.

Serene Cenote Xlacah in Dzibilchaltún

A DAY IN THE PUUC HILLS

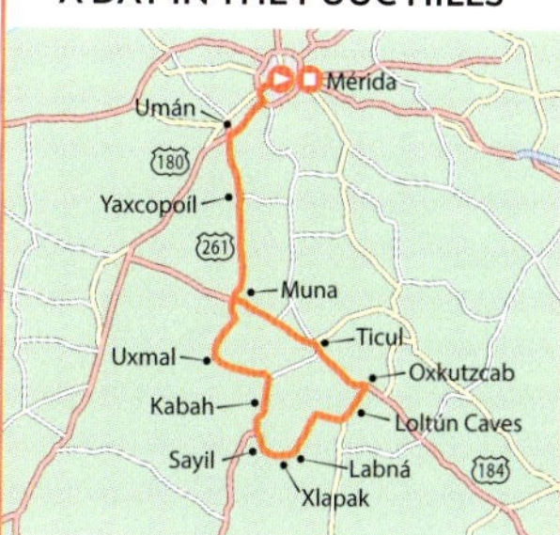

Morning

Leave **Mérida** *(p40)* early and drive directly to **Uxmal** *(p42)*. Beyond the suburb of Umán, where you turn onto Highway 261, traffic thins out, and it's an easy drive through woods and a few villages.

Beyond Muna the road enters the Puuc Hills before descending to Uxmal. Spend at least two hours exploring this site, and admiring the architecture.

Recoup your energies by heading back up the road to the nearby Hacienda Uxmal *(p121)* for *sopa de lima* on the terrace.

Afternoon

Head straight for **Kabah** to marvel at the monsters of the Codz Poop.

Further south, the "Puuc Route" turns off the main Highway 261 onto a lovely woodland road, with only a few other tourists, tricycle carts, and the birds for company. Along the way are stop-offs at the Puuc sites of **Sayil, Xlapak** *(p118)*, and **Labná** *(p115)*. At the end of the road, descend into the **Loltún Caves**, refreshing yourself afterward in the café.

Go down to **Oxkutzcab**, and turn left for **Ticul** *(p118)*, where you can take a stroll around its historic Plaza Mayor. Drive back to Mérida, stopping at **Yaxcopoíl** *(p118)* for a quick tour of the hacienda.

The Best of the Rest

Impressive ochre-colored church in Ticul

1. Oxkintok

B3 8:30am–5pm daily inah.gob.mx

This ancient Maya city has a Satunsat, or "Labyrinth" pyramid, containing a strange, dark maze, possibly built as an entrance to the Underworld that only the Lord of Oxkintok could use.

2. Yaxcopoíl Hacienda

C3 8am–6pm Mon–Sat, 9am–1pm Sun yaxcopoil.com

Of all the restored haciendas in the Yucatán, this one, with its crumbling, ornate main house and factory buildings, gives the best feel of life here when henequen or "green gold" dominated the state.

3. Cenotes

The cenotes and underwater rivers in the western Yucatán are far less well explored than those around Tulum *(p32)*. Snorkeling and diving trips are run from Mérida *(p40)*.

4. Chelem and Yucalpetén

C2

Just west of Progreso, on the other side of a gap in the coastal sand bar, these easygoing villages have long, almost empty beaches. They're popular for windsurfing.

5. Edzná

B5 8am–5pm daily (last adm: 4:30pm) inah.gob.mx

The ancient Maya town of Edzná is home to the "Building of the Five Stories," one of the largest Maya palaces in the region.

6. Ticul

C4

One of the most charming Yucatán country towns, Ticul is also a historic center for ceramics.

7. Acanceh

C3

On one side of the square of this remarkable little town is an 18th-century church, while on another is a very ancient Maya pyramid, perhaps begun around 300 BCE.

8. Mayapán

C3 8:30am–5pm daily inah.gob.mx

This was the last big Maya city, and one that dominated the Yucatán for 200 years after 1200. Its buildings often "mimic" Chichén Itzá and have beautifully preserved frescoes.

9. The Campeche Petenés

A4

This mangrove and forest wilderness is home to a wide range of wildlife, such as pumas and turtles. Trips can be taken from Campeche or the village of Isla Arena.

10. Xlapak

C4 8am–5pm daily inah.gob.mx

The smallest Puuc site *(p45)* is as attractive for the undisturbed woodland walk as for its archaeological site. The Palacio has intricate Puuc carving.

Places to Shop

1. Bazar de Artesanías Craft Market, Mérida

C2 Calle 67, by corner of Calle 56

This semi-official handicrafts market is packed with stalls selling every kind of Yucatecan and some excellent Mexican craftwork.

2. Casa de Artesanías, Mérida

C2 Calle 63, 503, between Calle 64 and Calle 66

The Yucatán state handicrafts store has high-quality local work, with many beautiful, usable things especially in textiles, basketware, and wood.

3. Mérida Market

C2 Calle 65, between Calle 54 and Calle 58

One of the world's greatest markets, this is a labyrinth of alleys and stalls selling everything imaginable – fish, fruit, a huge range of chilies, *huípil* blouses, sandals, and hats.

4. Hamacas La Poblana, Mérida

C2 Calle 65, 492, Centro

Street stalls sell low-quality but cheap hammocks – head here for the real thing in every color, size, and style, sold by weight.

5. El Charro Mexicano, Mérida

C2 Calle 59, 515, Zona Paseo Montejo, La Quinta

A little shop selling *botas* (boots) and *sombreros* (hats) opposite the market, with a friendly owner who will show you piles of handmade panamas in all sorts of styles and sizes.

6. Mexicanísimo, Mérida

C2 Parque Hidalgo Calle 60, between Calle 59 and Calle 61

This is an innovative store that sells lightweight clothes for men and women in original, modern designs, using Mexican cottons and other traditional materials.

7. Arte Maya, Ticul

C4 Calle 23, 301

Ticul produces huge quantities of ceramics. This family-run store stands out for the owners' skills and careful use of traditional and even ancient Maya techniques.

8. Guayaberas Jack, Mérida

C2 Calle 59, 507, between Calle 60 and Calle 62

The *guayabera* shirt-jacket is the smartest thing for gentlemen to wear in tropical Mérida. This long-established shop sells only *guayaberas*, and can make them to measure.

9. Maya Chuy Bordado, Mérida

C2 Calle 18, 80

This charming shop, tucked away from the crowded shopping streets of Mérida, is the outlet of a women's embroidery cooperative. Blouses, rugs, and other items are beautifully and individually made.

10. Casa de Artesanías Tukulná, Campeche

A5 Calle 10, 333, between Calle 59 and Calle 61

Campeche's state handicrafts store has a great choice of ceramics, embroidery, basketwork, and many other top-quality items that are beautifully displayed.

Colorful fresh produce on sale at Mérida Market

Bars and Cafés

Drinks behind the bar of La Negrita Cantina

1. La Fundación Mezcalería, Mérida

C2 Calle 59, 509, Parque Santa Lucia, Centro

This colorful spot specializes in mezcal-based cocktails. There's usually live or DJ-spun music.

2. Dulcería y Sorbetería El Colón, Mérida

C2 Calle 59, on the plaza

Choose from an excellent array of fruit-flavored sorbets and ice creams at this plaza-front parlor. A popular order is a *champola*, scoops of fruit ice served in a tall glass with milk.

3. La Negrita Cantina, Mérida

C2 Calle 62, 415 (999) 121 0411 Noon–10pm daily

Experience Havana at this bar, where the decor, drinks, and music all evoke this Caribbean city.

4. Café Crème, Mérida

C2 Calle 41, corner of Calle 60, Centro

Located in downtown Mérida, two blocks from Paseo Montejo, this café serves a variety of tasty French snacks and refreshing natural fruit juices.

5. Ku'uk, Mérida

C2 Av Rómulo Rozo No. 488, by Calle 27 and Calle 27A (999) 944 3377

Indulge in the tasting menu at this upscale restaurant or relax with a cocktail at its bar. There is also a fine collection of wine and beer, with many sourced from around Mexico.

6. Jugos California, Mérida

C2 Calle 58, 505 Centro

Juice stands are a wonderful local institution, and Jugos California wins the prize as the best in town. You'll find fresh watermelons, pineapples, papayas, and more here.

7. Piedra de Agua, Mérida

C2 Calle 62, 498

In a boutique hotel of the same name, close to the Santa Lucia church, this welcoming courtyard bar is a classy spot for an evening cocktail, glass of wine, or ice-cold beer.

8. Flamingos, Progreso

C2 Malecón, corner of Calle 22

One of Progreso's most enjoyable big terrace bar-restaurants, with tasty ceviches *(p75)* to go with the beer.

9. Casa Vieja de los Arcos, Campeche

A5 Calle 10, 319, Altos on the plaza

Watch the sun set from the balcony of this Cuban restaurant-bar on Campeche's central square. Enjoy their signature minty mojitos made with Cuban rum.

10. Nuevo Regis Cantina, Campeche

A5 Calle 12, 148, between 55 and 57

This traditional cantina is loved by locals for its low-key, relaxed atmosphere, and beer served in huge glasses.

Places to Eat

PRICE CATEGORIES

For a three-course meal for one with a beer or soda (or equivalent meal), taxes, and extra charges.

$ under US$15 $$ US$15–$35
$$$ over US$35

1. Amaro, Mérida

C2 Calle 59, 507, between Calle 60 and Calle 62 (999) 928 2451 · $$

One of old Mérida's loveliest patios houses this relaxing restaurant, which has a half-vegetarian menu, including several dishes made with *chaya (p75).*

2. El Marlín Azul, Mérida

C2 Calle 62, 488, between Calle 57 and Calle 59 (999) 928 1606 · $$

Ceviche is the dish to try at this seafood restaurant but don't miss the shrimp fajitas either.

3. El Príncipe Tutul-Xiu, Maní

C4 Calle 26, 208, between Calle 25 and Calle 27 (999) 929 7721 · $$

This restaurant is busiest on Sundays, when families drive from Mérida to eat *poc-chuc, panuchos,* and other Yucatecan staples *(p74).*

4. La Palapa, Celestún

A3 Calle 12, by corner of Calle 11 (988) 916 2063 · $$

La Palapa serves succulent platters of octopus, fish, and shrimp.

5. Ixi'im, Chocholá

A3 San Antonio Chablé, Chocholá · $$$

Ixi'im offers delicious Yucatecan cuisine in the charming setting of a former hacienda.

Diners enjoying a meal at La Chaya Maya

6. Hacienda Uxmal, Uxmal

C4 Antigua Carretera Mérida, Campeche, km 78 · $$$

This restaurant serves local and international cuisine in a tropical garden.

7. La Chaya Maya, Mérida

C2 Corner of Calle 62 and Calle 57, between Calle 60 and 62 · $$

An oasis of high-quality, reasonably priced Yucatecan food.

8. La Pigua, Campeche

A5 Alemán No. 179A · $$

Taking advantage of Campeche's prime position on the Gulf of Mexico, La Pigua serves fresh fish and seafood.

9. Casa de Piedra, Xcanatún

C2 Xcanatún, 7 miles (12 km) N of Mérida (999) 941 0213 · $$$

Casa de Piedra combines local and Caribbean cooking.

10. Hacienda San José Cholul

C2 Hwy Tixkokob–Tekanto, km 30 (999) 924 1333 · $$$

Set in a lovely colonial hacienda, the biggest draw is the secluded garden. The service is also excellent.

STREETSMART

A signpost near Cancún

7846 km
4875 mi
MARRUECOS
8406 km
5220 mi
ALEMANIA
XCARET
0 km
0 mi
7970 km
4952 mi
ESPAÑA
2527 km
1570 mi
ECUADOR
0 km
0 mi
XCARET

GETTING AROUND

Whether you're exploring Cancún on foot or by bike, or the Yucatán by car or public transportation, here is everything you need to know to navigate the region like a pro.

Arriving by Air

The Yucatán is served by several airports. Cancún Airport, 9 miles (15 km) south of Cancún, is the main international airport in the Yucatán. Direct flights depart daily from Canada and the US. From the UK or mainland Europe, you generally have to travel via the US or Mexico City, although there are a few scheduled flights and charter services during the high seasons. There are also airports in Cozumel, Tulum, and Mérida with daily international connections.

Colectivo minibuses are the easiest means of public transportation from the airports. In Cancún, they travel along the Hotel Zone and into Ciudad Cancún, dropping passengers at their hotel. Alternatively, reserve transportation in advance or use an airport cab; stands can be found as you exit most terminals.

There are also public transportation services from Cancún airport to various other destinations, including Puerto Morelos and Playa del Carmen.

Tren Maya

The **Tren Maya** launched in December 2024 to both fanfare and criticism *(p116)*. It now serves 34 stations covering 966 miles (1,554 km) across the states of Quintana Roo, Campeche, Tabasco, Chiapas, and the Yucatán, ferrying both locals and tourists around the region. This includes several stops by Maya sites – Palenque, Chichén Itzá, and Uxmal among them. Tours, ranging from four to six days, or tickets can be booked on the official website.

Children under five and those with certain disabilities travel for free. All trains also have spaces for wheelchair users as well as accessible bathrooms.

Tren Maya
W rutatrenmaya.com

Buses

Every city and most towns have a local bus service. Destinations are usually displayed on the windscreen, but

Cancún buses show route numbers. Buses are the main form of transportation for longer trips with providers such as **ADO**. First-class buses are air-conditioned and run between main cities and towns with only a few stops. Second-class buses are cheaper and stop more often. *Colectivos* (or *combis*) are minibuses that serve outlying districts and depart when full.

ADO
W ado.com.mx

Ferries

Passenger ferries run to Isla Mujeres from Puerto Juárez, which is just north of Cancún, every half hour or so daily. Fast boats will get you there in around 20 minutes. There are also several daily car ferries from Punta Sam.

Passenger ferries operated by **Ultramar** and **Winjet** run roughly every two hours between Playa del Carmen and Cozumel. The journey takes about 45 minutes. A Cozumel shuttle boat runs from Playa Tortugas in Cancún and there is a car ferry from Puerto Morelos, but it's infrequent and expensive.

Ultramar
W ultramarferry.com

Winjet
W winjet.mx

Taxis

Taxis in Cancún and the Yucatán don't tend to have meters, but instead charge official set rates for each locality. Note that cab drivers in some places, particularly Cancún, Playa del Carmen, and Tulum, have a reputation for charging foreigners inflated rates. Wherever you are going, always agree upon a price before getting into the cab.

In Cancún, there are different prices for the Hotel Zone and Ciudad Cancún. Official rates are far higher in the former.

Driving to Cancún and the Yucatán

When driving from the US you will need a Tourist Card to travel beyond the 12-mile (20-km) border zone and stay for more than 72 hours. You should also obtain Mexican insurance and a Temporary Import Permit for your vehicle, which is valid for six months. Allow five days to drive from the Texas border to the Yucatán. It's worth noting that most US car-rental companies will not allow their cars to be driven into Mexico. Bear in mind that the US-Mexico border, especially around Ciudad Juárez and Tijuana, is a hotspot in Mexico's drugs war, so it is essential to exercise extra caution. In most instances, it is easier to reach Mexico by plane, unless you're driving from within the country.

Driving in Cancún and the Yucatán

A car makes getting to the Maya sites and isolated beaches much easier. There are two fast toll highways in the Yucatán – the 180-Cuota, part of the route between Cancún and Mérida, and another stretch from Campeche to Champotón. Tolls are relatively high, so many drivers prefer the parallel old road (180–Libre). Note that *topes*, or speed bumps, are common and can often be hard to spot.

In rural areas, there are few gas stations, so make sure you fill up when you can. Occasionally, station attendants start the pump with pesos already on the gauge. To avoid this, get out of the car and check the pump is set at zero.

Car Rental

There are plenty of rental offices in the Riviera Maya, but if you are traveling around the Yucatán, it is best to rent in Mérida, whose smaller agencies tend to be cheaper. To rent a car you must be over 21 and have your driving license, passport, and a credit card.

Walking

Old Yucatán cities such as Mérida, Campeche, and Valladolid are fairly compact and generally safe, and strolling around is the best way to get to know them. Mechanized transportation is only really essential in Cancún.

PRACTICAL INFORMATION

A little local know-how goes a long way in Cancún and the Yucatán. On these pages you can find all the essential advice and information you will need to make the most of your trip to the region.

ELECTRICITY SUPPLY

Standard voltage is 127 volts. Power sockets across Mexico are type A and B, fitting plugs with two flat pins.

Passports and Visas

For entry requirements, including visas, consult your nearest Mexican embassy or check with the **Mexican Department of Foreign Relations**. All travelers to Mexico need a passport that is valid for six months longer than their intended period of stay.

Citizens of the US, Canada, the UK, Australia, New Zealand, and the Schengen region do not need visas to enter Mexico as tourists for fewer than 180 days.

Mexican Department of Foreign Relations
W portales.sre.gob.mx/guiadeviaje

Government Advice

Now more than ever, it is important to consult both your and the Mexican government's advice before traveling. The UK Foreign, Commonwealth and Development Office (**FCDO**), the **US Department of State**, the **Australian Department of Foreign Affairs and Trade**, and **Gobierno de Mexico** offer the latest information on security, health, and local regulations.

Australian Department of Foreign Affairs and Trade
W smartraveller.gov.au
FCDO
W gov.uk/foreign-travel-advice
Gobierno de Mexico
W gob.mx/sre/en
US Department of State
W travel.state.gov

Customs Information

You can find information on the laws relating to goods and currency taken in or out of Mexico on the Gobierno de México's **Aduanas** website.

Aduanas
W anam.gob.mx/pasajeros

Insurance

We recommend that you take out a comprehensive insurance policy covering theft, loss of belongings, medical care, cancelations, and delays, and read the small print carefully.

If you plan to go scuba diving you may need additional coverage.

Vaccinations

No inoculations are required for visiting Mexico, but all travelers are advised to seek immunization against typhoid, tetanus, polio, hepatitis A, hepatitis B, diphtheria, and rabies. If you are heading into forest or jungle areas elsewhere in Mexico or Central America, consult your doctor about malaria pills.

Money

Most major credit and debit cards are accepted almost everywhere. Contactless payments are increasingly common; however, small businesses, street food stands, and market vendors prefer cash (or accept it exclusively) and/or charge a fee for paying by card. It is worth carrying cash for smaller items and tips, and smaller denominations are recommended, as many vendors are unable to make change for large bills.

All tourist areas have small foreign-exchange offices *(cambios)* and banks generally have an ATM, although they can be hard to find in rural areas. Some businesses on the Riviera accept US dollars. Note, though, that USD prices usually work out higher than pesos.

A tip of 15–20 percent is expected in restaurants and bars, and hotel porters and housekeeping will expect a tip of $10–20 per bag or day. At major resorts, additional tips are expected: $20–50 per day for housekeeping and $50–100 for the concierge.

Travelers with Specific Requirements

Larger hotels and resorts in Cancún and Cozumel often have good wheelchair facilities, although those in older buildings can be difficult to access. Always check before booking.

Public transportation provisions for those with physical disabilities are poor. Buses and ferries are rarely wheelchair-accessible, but drivers are usually helpful. The slow ferries to Isla Mujeres are easier to board thanks to ramps. Sidewalks in Cancún also have wheelchair ramps at street junctions.

Most of the region's ancient Maya sites have steps and narrow, stony paths, and are not well equipped for travelers with disabilities. Only larger sites, such as Chichén Itzá and Uxmal, have relatively smooth walkways that are accessible.

Organizations including **Yucatek Divers** in Playa del Carmen and **Cancún Accesible** offer tours and transportation for those with specific requirements. It is also recommended to consult online resources such as **México Accesible** for detailed advice.

Cancún Accesible
W cancunaccesible.com

México Accesible
W accesiblemexico.com

Yucatek Divers
W yucatek-divers.com

Language

Spanish is the official language spoken in Mexico. In the Yucatán region, more than half a million residents speak an Indigenous language and you are likely to hear one or more of these languages. English, however, is spoken widely, particularly in resort areas.

Opening Hours

Most shops open around 8:30am and close at 9pm from Monday to Saturday, with the more traditional ones closing for lunch 1–3pm. Markets open very early, before 8am, and close by 2–3pm.

Banks are usually open 8:30am–4pm Monday to Friday, and 9am–1pm on Saturday; some won't exchange money in the afternoons or on Saturdays.

Situations can change quickly and unexpectedly. Always check before visiting attractions and hospitality venues for up-to-date opening hours and booking requirements.

Personal Security

The Yucatán is generally safe, but petty crime does occur. Be wary of pickpocketing especially in Cancún, Mérida, and Playa del Carmen. Use your common sense, leave valuables in a hotel safe, and be alert to your surroundings. There have been incidents of sexual assault against female travelers in resort areas; avoid walking alone late at night or in the early morning. If you have anything stolen or experience crime, report the incident as soon as possible to the local police department. Be sure to obtain a copy of the crime report to claim on your insurance. Contact your embassy or consulate if your passport is stolen or in the event of a serious incident.

As a rule, Mexicans are accepting of all people. Same-sex marriage was legalized in the region in 2021 and discrimination on the basis of sexual orientation is illegal. As such, the LGBTQ+ community is becoming more prominent, especially in urban areas, but there may still be a degree of prejudice in rural communities. **Gay Mexico Map** lists LGBTQ+ bars, clubs, and hotels in areas throughout the country.

Gay Mexico Map
W gaymexicomap.com

AT A GLANCE

EMERGENCY NUMBER

GENERAL EMERGENCY

911

TIME ZONE

While Cancún is on Eastern Standard Time (EST), the Yucatán is on Central Standard Time (CST).

TAP WATER

Tap water is not potable and visitors are advised to drink bottled or treated water only.

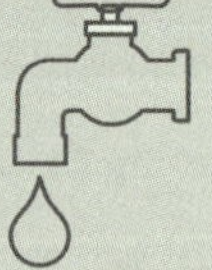

WEBSITES AND APPS

Cancún website
The official visitor website for Cancún *(turismocancun.mx)* includes pages of information and links for visitors.

Yucatán website
Official visitor website for the Yucatán *(yucatan.travel/en)*, providing plenty of useful tourist information.

ADO App
The official app for bus travel across the region. Allows visitors to book bus tickets and offers a cheaper rate than booking elsewhere

Health

Healthcare in Mexico, especially at private facilities, is generally good; however, medical travel insurance is recommended to cover costs related to an accident or sudden illness. You may need to pay for treatment upfront and reclaim the money later from your insurance company. Should you be in a serious accident, an ambulance will pick you up and may charge on the spot.

Private clinics in larger cities may employ English-speaking staff. For minor ailments, however, it's still advisable to seek advice from one of the local pharmacies *(farmacias)*. Many are open 24 hours a day in large cities and have an on-site doctor. In small towns and rural areas, basic health centers *(centros de salud)* have emergency facilities.

Smoking, Alcohol, and Drugs

Mexico has strict smoking legislation. Smoking and vaping are prohibited in all public places, whether indoors or outdoors. Enforcement may be erratic, but fines can be stiff for those caught.

You must be 18 to drink or purchase alcohol. It's illegal to walk the streets with an open container of alcohol.

Recreational cannabis is a complicated matter in Mexico. The Supreme Court decriminalized the personal use of cannabis in 2021, but the legal and licensing procedures for its sale and consumption have still not been actualized. Travelers are advised to forego using cannabis. Some prescription medicine may also be regarded as illegal drugs, so bring a letter from your doctor or your prescription to prove these are for prescribed use only.

ID

Passports are required as ID at airports. It is advisable to take copies of your passport when traveling between cities by bus or if driving a car since there are frequent police checkpoints.

Responsible Travel

The Yucatán Peninsula (and Mexico as a whole) is suffering from water scarcity. Do your bit by avoiding long showers, and reusing towels if staying in a hotel. You can also cut back on single-use plastic through taking a water purifier with you from home.

At the beach, use biodegradable and reef-safe sunscreen, to minimize your impact on marine environments.

When visiting sacred sites always be respectful of local traditions, history, and culture. Turn off your cell phone and only take photographs (including of people) if permitted.

Cell Phones and Wi-Fi

If you plan to use your cell phone in Mexico, consult your service provider before arriving to check for tariffs. Calls can be expensive so consider purchasing a Mexican SIM card once you've arrived.

High-speed internet is generally widely available throughout Mexico, especially in the cities. Increasingly, cities are providing free Wi-Fi in public spaces, and many cafés, restaurants, and businesses offer free Wi-Fi.

Postal Services

Mexico's postal service is run by **Correos de México**. Main post offices *(oficinas de correos)* are open from 8am to 8pm on weekdays, and from 8am to 3pm on Saturdays. Smaller sites often have shorter opening hours. For international services it is best to use DHL or FedEx.

Correos de México
W correosdemexico.com.mx

Taxes and Refunds

Prices usually include 16 percent sales tax. If a price is given as *más IVA* (plus sales tax) it means that 16 percent will be added to the bill. Visitors can claim a refund upon exiting Mexico, so save your receipts if you wish to do this.

Visitors to the state of Quintana Roo are also charged a tourist tax known as the **Visitax**. The tax is 224 Mexican pesos (roughly US$12) per person.

Visitax
W visitax.gob.mx/sitiol

Trips and Tours

Tours are a great way to see cities, Maya sites, jungle wildlife, and so on. Most large cities have bus tours that leave from central areas, including the Paseo Turístico in Mérida, and the Tranvía de la Ciudad and El Guapo tours in Campeche.

Many companies offer guided tours to the main Maya sites, with **Mayan Heritage** in Mérida among the best. Choose your tour carefully as some companies don't allow more than a few hours on-site, and often arrive during the hottest part of the day. Larger sites have official guides on-site, who can show you round for an hourly fee and are often highly informative.

A variety of ecotour operators offer trips to sites such as Sian Ka'an Biosphere Reserve *(p34)* and specialize in nature and bird-watching tours. A list of these can be found on the **Yucatan Wildlife** website.

Mayan Heritage
W mayanheritage.com.mx
Yucatan Wildlife
W yucatanwildlife.com

PLACES TO STAY

Whether you're a budget traveler or you're looking to splurge, Cancún and the Yucatán have accommodations for every price point. All-inclusive resorts abound in Cancún and the Riviera Maya, while boutique hotels, historic hacienda estates, and independently owned properties dot the interior towns.

Be sure to book ahead during peak times (typically Dec–Apr and Jul–Sep), and especially for Semana Santa (Holy Week). This usually coincides with the US Spring Break and prices will substantially increase.

PRICE CATEGORIES

For a standard double room per night (with breakfast if included), taxes, and extra charges.

$ under US$70
$$ US$70–$150
$$$ over US$150

Cancún and the North

Ser Casasandra

G1 Calle Igualdad, Isla Holbox casasandra.com · $$$

A project by the Cuban artist Sandra Pérez, Casasandra ("Sandra's home") is all about understated luxury. The 17 rooms (and one villa) eschew gaudy features found in many resorts, instead there are terra-cotta floors, responsibly sourced furnishings, and artworks by Mexican artists and Pérez herself.

St. Regis Kanai

R4 Av Benito Juárez s/n, playa del Carmen marriott.com · $$$

This branch of the St. Regis combines all the amenities you'd expect from a five-star brand – butler service, numerous swimming pools, and over 10,000 ft (3,050 m) of spa space – with great environmental projects. These include beach clean-ups, producing its own water, and protecting the 400-year-old mangrove forest the hotel sits above.

Mayan Monkey Cancún

K4 Blvd. Kukulcan, km 9.5, Zona Hotelera, Cancún mayanmonkey.com · $

Choose between dorms or private rooms at this affordable hostel, in the Hotel Zone of Cancún. There are plenty of on-site activities to choose from, including cocktail classes, game nights, and yoga, and the friendly staff can hook you up with regional tours.

Waldorf Astoria Cancún

R3 Carretera Federal Libre 307 Cancún-Tulum, Cancún waldorfastoriacancun.com · $$$

With so much to do at this 2022 addition to Cancún's hotel scene, you may find it hard to justify leaving the vast 100-acre (40-hectare) hotel. Spend days being pampered in the Maya-inspired spa, lounging on the private beach, or engaging in the watersports offered here. Don't worry about finding a room with a view – they all include a balcony overlooking the ocean.

Hotel Adhara Cancún

J3 Av Carlos Nader 1–2, Mz 3, Cancún adharacancun.com · $$

Want to enjoy Cancún away from tourists in the Hotel Zone? Book this hotel located in Ciudad Cancún. It's just a short walk from the Mercado 23 *(p90)* and many of the other sites in Downtown. And despite its lower price, the Adhara still has plenty of great amenities, including an on-site gym, pool, bar, and restaurant.

Vidanta Mayan Palace

R4 Carretera Cancún-Playa del Carmen, km 48 vidanta.com/web/riviera-maya · $$$

If you're looking to stay in the lap of luxury, look no further than here. The Mayan Palace has everything: an elegant spa, 20 world-class restaurants, a wide range of activities, and bookable excursions. It even hosts the world-famous Cirque du Soleil throughout the year in a purpose-built venue located in the jungle.

Hotel Secreto

L1 Sección Lote 11, Isla Mujeres W hotelsecreto.com · $$

Hidden away on the far side of Isla Mujeres, this small hotel exudes peace and tranquility, despite being just minutes from the center of town. There are only 12 rooms, which adds to the sense of calm, and all include four-poster beds, wooden furnishings, and abstract artworks. Book a suite to have your own balcony overlooking the pool and beach.

Etéreo

Q4 Paseo Kanai 16, Playa del Carmen W aubergeresorts.com · $$

White sandy beaches, a relaxing spa, a superb on-site restaurant, and decadent rooms "floating" over a mangrove forest, this Auberge outpost has everything needed for a luxurious stay. If all this isn't enough, check out the list of activities here, including cooking classes, volleyball, soccer, pickleball, and a fun kids' club.

Rancho Sak-Ol

R3 Mz 1 Lotte, Puerto Morelos W ranchosakol.com · $

Few hotels build a sense of community like this Puerto Morales spot – you'll feel it most at breakfast, which is often a communal effort in the shared kitchen. Afterward, escape to nearby Cancún or use the complimentary bikes to get to the best local spots, before reconvening for sundowners at the hotel's beachfront bar.

Cozumel and the South

Copal Tulum

P6 Calle Ixchel, corner of Av Juaneh Aldea Zamá, Tulúm W copaltulumhotel.com · $$

Tucked into a tangle of trees and foliage, the Copal may feel a little away from the action, but it's worth the trip thanks to the staff. No task is too much for the team here, who manage to make every stay memorable through their attentiveness and local knowledge, which makes planning excursions a piece of cake.

Lula

G4 Carretera Tulum Boca Paila, km 8.1, Tulum W lulahoteltulum.com · $$

If martial art classes, beachfront yoga, and a relaxing spa sound like your kind of holiday, look no further. This shoreline hotel outside of Tulum has all the wellness amenities you could ask for, and you'll feel even better knowing the site uses responsible environmental practices.

Hotel B Cozumel

R5 Carretera Playa San Juan, km 2.5, Cozumel W hotelbcozumel.com · $$$

Travelers who want to spend their days on the water should book this hotel. It's set in a natural bay that's perfect for snorkelers and swimmers of all ages, as well as more adventurous activities such as diving, kayaking, and kite-surfing. If you want even calmer waters, laze about in the hotel pool that overlooks the Caribbean Sea.

Amigo's Hostel

R5 Calle 7 Sur 571, Cozumel (987) 119 9664 · $

This friendly hostel is among the most affordable stays in Cozumel, with spacious shared areas, comfy dorms, and a well-equipped kitchen. But what sets it apart is the owner, Kathy, who might just provide the best service on the island. She is incredibly friendly and a fount of local knowledge, such as where to find the best beaches and restaurants, where to shop, and which Cozumel tours to take.

Presidente InterContinental Cozumel Resort & Spa

R5 Carretera A Chankanaab, km 6.5, Cozumel W presidenteiccozumel.com · $$$

Not many hotels can claim to have either their own marina or a stretch of private, white-sand beach, but this grand dame of Cozumel has both. Choose between relaxing in luxury on the beach or in the hotel spa, or head out with the on-site dive center to explore the nearby coral reef.

Aqua Viva

Calle 33, Mz 4, corner of Calle 32, Bacalar aquaviva.mx · $$

This place close to Lake Bacalar proves exclusivity doesn't have to break the bank. You'll pay less than for a resort but stay in your own villa decked out in all the hi-tech mod-cons imaginable. Every detail has been thought of, from the well-stocked kitchen and excellent gym to the attentive staff who can help with everything from laundry to arranging excursions.

Casa Hormiga

Av 3 corner of Calle 32, Mario Villanueva Madrid, Bacalar casahormiga.com · $$

This environmentally friendly boutique hotel is perfect for those in need of some self-care. The hotel specializes in transformative experiences centered on the senses and natural elements: water, earth, fire, air, and ether. After your ritual, enjoy a Middle Eastern and Mexican fusion meal in the hotel restaurant.

The Central Heartland

Hacienda San José Cholul

C2 Carretera Tixhokob-Tekanto, Km 30, Tixhokob ihg.com · $$$

Sitting in a restored Maya estate, this manor has the perfect conditions for a relaxing escape. After a free drink at check in, laze about in a hammock suspended over the pool or enjoy a specialist treatment at the spa (which is also plastic free). It doesn't get better than this.

Hotel Waye

E3 Calle 41, 52 and 54, Valladolid waye.mx · $

You get a lot of bang for your buck at this budget-friendly Valladolid hotel. The 22 rooms are all spacious and range from standard rooms with plush beds to suites that include a private terrace and jacuzzi. All rooms are decorated with locally made textiles and quirky crafts, such as colorful wooden masks.

Hotel Cenote Secreto Maya

F3 Carretera Yalcoba–XTut, km 9 cenotesecretomaya.com.mx · $$$

A cabin just steps away from a 66-million-year-old cenote? *Sí, por favor!* Guests enjoy special nighttime swimming privileges in the 175-ft- (54-m-) deep pool before drying off around a fire pit. During the day, you can use the inflatables and rope swing in the cenote, or even rappel down into the cavern.

Hotel Hacienda de Izamal

D2 Calle 38, 284, 19 and 21, Izamal haciendadeizamal.com · $

This budget-friendly hotel may be a little more basic than others, but it has the most desirable location in Izamal: all of the city's major attractions are within easy walking distance, along with the best local restaurants. If you don't fancy walking, grab one of the bikes offered at the front desk – they're a great way to explore the city.

Hacienda Chichén & Yaxkin Spa

E3 Zona Hotelera de Chichén Itzá, km 120, carretera libre 180-Puerto Juárez haciendachichen.com · $$

If you want to beat the crowds to Chichén Itzá, book a stay at this old hacienda located next to the Maya site itself (and with its own entrance to Chichén). Not that it's just about Maya history. No, the hotel is set in a vast nature reserve and helps to preserve local wildlife and endemic flora.

The West

Hacienda Xcanatún

C2 Calle 20 s/n, Xcanatún, Mérida angsana.com/mexico/hacienda-xcanatun · $$$

This beautifully restored hacienda was originally a colonial estate, and you certainly won't lack for space. Step outside and you'll find four acres (two hectares) of lush gardens, packed with endemic plants and trees, and an Olympic-sized pool. It's equally spacious inside, with 18 historic suites dating back to the 18th century and 36 modern suites, which blend traditional materials with a contemporary design.

Art 57

C2 Calle 57 543, Barrio de Santiago, Mérida art57hotel.com · $

In a city filled with pricey hotels, Art 57 is a welcome budget-friendly option. It has comfortable, well-appointed rooms and is colorful throughout, thanks to the local Mexican artists who have decorated the spaces. It even has a junior suite with a private pool if you're looking for a small splurge.

The Diplomat Boutique Hotel

C2 Calle 78, 493A, by 59 and 59a, Mérida thediplomatmerida.com · $$$

The Canadian couple who own this chic hotel spent two decades traveling all over the world together and their experiences inform the design of this place. It's filled with carefully selected antiques and artifacts, and guests can purchase their own keepsake at the on-site shop selling locally crafted goods.

Boutique by the Museo

C2 Calle 58 and 43, 481, Mérida boutiquebythemuseo.com · $$$

Few hotels are as ideal for families as this boutique. Almost all rooms come with two or three bedrooms and the hotel organizes day trips and cooking classes. Best of all, as the name suggests, it's close to a museum (Museo de Antropología), where you can learn about the Maya world.

Hacienda Temozón Sur

C3 Carretera Mérida-Uxmal, km 182, Temozón Sur ihg.com · $$$

History lovers will adore this hacienda, which was once a sisal-producing farm. The hotel retains many original features: think hardwood antique furniture, tiled floors, soaring 18-ft- (5-m-) high ceilings, and a famously deep-red exterior. All of the 28 rooms here are named after their original functions, including a school and a pharmacy.

Hacienda Uxmal Plantation & Museum

C4 Highway Mérida Cancún, km 120 mayaland.com · $$

Join the likes of Queen Elizabeth II and Jackie Kennedy in booking a stay at this hacienda; dating back to 1683, it's supposedly the oldest such building in the world. There are even more historical tales to uncover across the road, at the Maya city of Uxmal.

Playa 55 Beach Escape

A3 Calle 12, Benito Juárez, Celestún playa55beachescape.com · $$$

This adults-only beachfront property was acquired by a Canadian couple who previously worked in interior design. They have worked their magic here, filling the place with a cool locally inspired design, custom arts and crafts, and unique touches like a traditional hammock in each room and an outdoor fire ring (lit upon request). The beach is just outside and it's lovely.

Hacienda Puerta Campeche

A5 Calle 59, 71 between 16 and 18, Campeche ihg.com · $$$

Set in a former 16th-century convent, this atmospheric hacienda promises spacious rooms and a sun-drenched pool that ingeniously flows through the historical, but now roofless, stone-walled rooms. Swim from the lobby to your room for a siesta in a cotton-woven hammock.

Hacienda Uayamón

B5 Carretera China-edzna Uayamón, km 20 ihg.com · $$$

Need an escape from the urban bustle? Then this rural former henequen plantation is for you. Guests can wander the peaceful grounds, which are full of crumbling colonial buildings, or be revitalized in the spa, which uses natural products made with ancient Maya methods. Be sure to book a meal at the on-site restaurant to enjoy superb local favorites while overlooking old sisal-factory ruins.

INDEX

Page numbers in **bold** refer to main entries.

C

O

P

Q

R

S

PHRASE BOOK

In an Emergency

Help!	¡Socorro! ¡Auxilio!	soh-koh-roh o-xe-leo
Call a doctor!	¡Llame a un médico!	yah-meh ah oon meh-dee-koh
Call an ambulance!	¡Llame una ambulancia!	yah-meh ah oonah ahm-boo-lahn-see-ah
Call the fire department!	¡Llame a los bomberos!	yah-meh ah lohs bohm-beh-rohs
Police officer	el policía!	ehl poh-lee-see-ah

Communication Essentials

Yes	Sí	see
No	No	noh
Please	Por favor	pohr fah-vohr
Thank you	Gracias	grah-see-ahs
Excuse me	Perdone	pehr-doh-neh
Hello	Hola	oh-lah
Bye (casual)	Chau	chau
Goodbye	Adiós	ah-dee-ohs
What?	¿Qué?	keh
When?	¿Cuándo?	kwahn-doh
Why?	¿Por qué?	pohr-keh
Where?	¿Dónde?	dohn-deh
How are you?	¿Cómo está usted?	koh-moh ehs-tah oos-tehd
Very well, thank you	Muy bien, gracias	mwee bee-ehn grah-see-ahs
I'm sorry	Lo siento	loh see-ehn-toh

Useful Phrases

Where is/are…?	¿Dónde está/están…?	dohn-deh ehs-tah/ehs-tahn
How far is it to…?	¿Cuántos metros/ kilómetros hay de aquí a…?	kwahn-tohs meh-trohs/kee-loh-meh-trohs eye deh ah-kee ah
Which way is it to…?	¿Por dónde se va a…?	pohr dohn-deh seh vah ah
Do you speak English?	¿Habla inglés?	ah-blah een-glehs
I don't understand	No comprendo/ entiendo	noh kohm-prehn-doh
I would like	Quisiera/ Me gustaría	kee-see-yehr-ah meh goo-stah-ree ah

Useful Words

big	grande	grahn-deh
small	pequeño/a	peh-keh-nyoh/nyah
hot	caliente	kah-lee-ehn-teh
cold	frío/a	free-oh/ah
good	bueno/a	bweh-noh/nah
bad	malo/a	mah-loh/lah
open	abierto/a	ah-bee-ehr-toh/tah
closed	cerrado/a	sehr-rah-doh/dah
left	izquierda	ees-key-ehr-dah
right	derecha	deh-reh-chah
(keep) straight ahead	(siga) derecho	(see-gah) deh-reh-choh
near	cerca	sehr-kah
far	lejos	leh-hohs
more	más	mahs
less	menos	meh-nohs
entrance	entrada	ehn-trah-dah
exit	salida	sah-lee-dah
elevator	el ascensor	ehl ah-sehn-sohr
toilets	baños/	bah-nyohs/
women's	de damas	deh dah-mahs
men's	de caballeros	deh kah-bah-yeh-rohs

Post Offices and Banks

Where can I change money?	¿Dónde puedo cambiar dinero?	dohn-deh pweh-doh kahm-bee-ahr dee-neh-roh
How much is the postage to…?	¿Cuánto cuesta enviar una carta a…?	kwahn-toh kweh-stah ehn-vee-yahr oo-nah kahr-tah ah
I need stamps	Necesito estampillas	neh-seh-see-toh ehs-tahm-pee-yah

Shopping

How much does this cost?	¿Cuánto cuesta esto?	kwahn-toh kwehs-tah ehs-toh
I would like…	Me gustaría…	meh goos-tah-ree-ah
Do you have?	¿Tienen?	tee-yeh-nehn
Do you take credit cards	¿Aceptan tarjetas de crédito	ahk-sehp-tahn tahr-heh-tahs deh kreh-dee-toh
expensive	caro	kahr-oh
cheap	barato	bah-rah-toh
budget friendly	económico	eh-koh-noh-mee-koh
white	blanco	blahn-koh
black	negro	neh-groh
red	rojo	roh-hoh
yellow	amarillo	ah-mah-ree-yoh
green	verde	vehr-deh
blue	azul	ah-sool
bakery	la panadería	lah pah-nah-deh ree-ah
bank	el banco	ehl bahn-koh
bookstore	la librería	lah lee-breh-ree-ah
market	el tianguis/ mercado	ehl tee-ahn-goo-ees/mehr-kah-doh
post office	la oficina de correos	lah oh-fee-see-nah deh kohr-reh-ohs
supermarket	el supermercado	ehl soo-pehr-mehr-kah-doh
travel agency	la agencia de viajes	lah ah-hehn-see-ah ah deh vee-ah-hehs

Transportation

When does the… leave?	¿A qué hora sale el…?	ah keh oh-rah sah-leh ehl
Where is the bus stop?	¿Dónde está la parada de buses?	dohn-deh ehs-tah lah pah-rah-dah deh boo-sehs
Is there a bus/ train to…?	¿Hay un camión/tren a…?	eye oon kah-mee-ohn/trehn ah…?
platform	el andén	ehl ahn-dehn
ticket office	la taquilla	lah tah-kee-yah
round-trip ticket	un boleto de ida y vuelta	oon boh-leh-toh deh ee-dah ee voo-ehl-tah
one-way ticket	un boleto de ida solamente	oon boh-leh-toh deh ee-dah soh-lah-mehn-teh
airport	el aeropuerto	ehl ah-ehr-oh-poo-ehr-toh
Taxi stand/rank	sitio de taxis	see-tee-oh deh tahk-sees

Sightseeing

beach	la playa	lah plah-yah
cathedral	la catedral	lah kah-teh-drahl
church	la iglesia/ la basílica	lah ee-gleh-see-ah/ lah bah-see-lee-kah
garden	el jardín	ehl hahr-deen
museum	el museo	ehl moo-seh-oh
pyramid	la pirámide	lah pee-rah-meed
ruins	las ruinas	lahs roo-ee-nahs

Gerasimovvv 20tc; Vlad Ghiea 29br; Sergio Hayashi 73br; Patryk Kosmider 26br; Jesse Kraft 35br; Loeskieboom 69bl; Mariakray 28–29t, 66b, 86–87tc; Ronniechua 64–65b; SimonDannhauer 17b; Sl Photography 16tl, 115tr, Enrique Gomez Tamez 58–59; Prakich Treetasayuth 45b; Joanne Weston 32cl.

Getty Images: Moment / © Marco Bottigelli 5; Tramino 105br; Universal Images Group / Education Images 15tr.

Getty Images / iStock: Simon Dannhauer 56–57t; E+ / Swissmediavision 32–33b, 50–51bc; Mariakray 10clb; Domingo Saez Romero 15bc; Jonathan Ross 22–23t; Arkadij Schell 26bl; SCStock 46–47t; SL_Photography 13tl; YinYang 13clb.

La Parrilla: 93br.

Shutterstock.com: Aberu.Go 96–97bc; Marco Bicci 24b; Yingna Cai 63t; Feelthedrone 27t; Nekomura 80b; Pack-Shot 16ca; Pixel-Shot 75tl.

Cover images:

Front and Spine: **Getty Images:** Moment / Eduardo Fonseca Arraes.
Back: **Alamy Stock Photo:** Eric Galton tl; Greg Vaughn tr; **Dreamstime.com:** Sorin Colac cl.

Sheet Map Cover Image:

Getty Images: Moment / Eduardo Fonseca Arraes.

A NOTE FROM DK

The rate at which the world is changing is constantly keeping the DK travel team on our toes. While we've worked hard to ensure that this edition of Cancún and the Yucatán is accurate and up-to-date, we know that opening hours alter, standards shift, prices fluctuate, places close and new ones pop up in their stead. So, if you notice we've got something wrong or left something out, we want to hear about it.Please get in touch at travelguides@dk.com

Within each Top 10 list in this book, no hierarchy of quality or popularity is implied. All 10 are, in the editor's opinion, of roughly equal merit.

First edition 2003

Published in Great Britain by Dorling Kindersley Limited, DK, 20 Vauxhall Bridge Road, London SW1V 2SA

The authorised representative in the EEA is Dorling Kindersley Verlag GmbH. Arnulfstr. 124, 80636 Munich, Germany

Published in the United States by DK Publishing, 1745 Broadway, 20th Floor, New York, NY 10019, USA

25 26 27 28 10 9 8 7 6 5 4 3 2 1

A CIP catalog record for this book is available from the British Library.

A catalog record for this book is available from the Library of Congress.

ISSN: 1479-344X
ISBN: 978 0 2417 5747 5

Printed and bound in China

www.dk.com

This book was made with Forest Stewardship Council™ certified paper – one small step in DK's commitment to a sustainable future.
Learn more at **www.dk.com/uk/information/sustainability**